THE EFFECTIVE
SUPERVISOR

THE EFFECTIVE
SUPERVISOR

John Adair

First published in March 1988 by

The Industrial Society
Peter Runge House
3 Carlton House Terrace
London
SW1Y 5DG

ISBN 1 85091 569 5

British Library Cataloguing in Publication Data

Adair, John *1934*

The Effective Supervisor.
1. Supervision of employees
I. Title
658 3' 02   HF5549

personnel management
Supervisory Studies

Printed and bound in Great Britain by
Biddles Ltd, Guildford and King's Lynn

CONTENTS

INTRODUCTION

This book is a comprehensive guide to the practice of good management at the first-line level. Too often such jobs have been given to those who are technically or professionally competent but who lack interest in people or skills in dealing with them. The message of this book is that leadership, communication and problem-solving skills lie at the core of the supervisor's role.

Are leaders born or made? There is no doubt that — given a certain basic potential — leadership can be developed. The first step, of course, is to want to be a better leader. Granted that is the frame of mind in which you approach this book you should find that it will provide you with a much clearer concept of the role and key responsibilities of a supervisor, together with some guidelines on how to make it all happen in practice, well illustrated by examples and cases.

The introductory chapter focuses on you — the effective supervisor. It defines a supervisor and highlights the strategic importance of good first-line management in any organisation today. It emphasises leadership as the heart of the matter, for management is about getting results with and through people. Leadership means enabling a group to achieve its common task, building it into a high-performance team and developing, training and motivating each individual member. But you do not have to do it all yourself. A good supervisor will delegate to others. That should leave you with time to think and plan ahead.

Chapter 2 highlights the importance of communication, which is inseparable from leadership. The key skills of speaking and listening are obviously required, but this chapter looks also at the relevant systems of communication, especially team briefing. This is a system that ensures that each supervisor will get his or her team together on a regular basis to brief them on progress and policy as well as matters which affect their welfare or development as employees. As the effective supervisor has a stake in good organisational communication, the chapter briefly surveys other methods or forms of communication which ought to be of use in an organisation.

Leadership is not about seeking popularity. If a leader is respected that is enough; if esteem develops that must be regarded as a pleasing bonus. But true leaders will have the moral courage to face and deal with unpleasant situations. The right policies and skills required to take disciplinary action are set out in Chapter 3.

Of all the problems facing a supervisor, absenteeism can be one of the most vexing. After all, if people fail to turn up to work you do not have a team. Chapter 4 explores the nature of absenteeism, causes of the problem and how to go about tackling it. Part of the solution lies outside the supervisor's hands, but it is amazing what effect the leader can have on the simple issue of whether or not people resolve to come in to work when they are tempted (by excuses rather than real reasons) to stay at home. Ultimately organisations will find it difficult to employ those who are not both highly motivated and self-motivated.

Both your organisation and you as a supervisor will never have a second chance to make a first impression. Induction, the subject of Chapter 5, is crucial in two ways. The new recruit will form his or her first and most abiding impressions of the organisation during the induction period; equally, the organisation, through you as its immediate representative, can integrate the new person swiftly into the team. That means, of course, giving them a considerable amount of information about aims and objectives, as well as answering the questions which all new people have when they join an organisation — especially concerning the jobs and opportunities for training and development.

You may like to show the 'open letter' in Chapter 6 to your boss! Leadership can be exercised upwards as well as downwards and sideways. You may have to influence your boss and the organisation to see their supervisor in a different light, to invert the hierarchical pyramid and see that the managers closest to the front line really are the leaders upon whom excellence of product and service, business performance and the job satisfaction of intelligent and highly motivated employees have come to depend. I hope this book will help you to change the unhelpful attitudes and limited expectations which still characterise the relations of second-rate managers with their supervisors.

The chapter entitled 'The Supervisor as a Professional Manager' explores in further depth those central three overlapping areas of leadership responsibility: achieving the task, building the team and developing the individual. It underlines the need, too, for proper training for supervisory leadership. Would you entrust your children to a bus driver who had had no training in how to drive a bus? Of course not. Yet we entrust our work people to supervisors who have had no specific training in the general personal skills required for first-line management. That is fair neither to the work people concerned nor to the supervisor who is being pitchforked into the job. In this chapter I have given some character sketches of bad supervisors to make the point.

The subject of industrial relations is addressed in Chapter 7. As I see it, the shop steward is there to promote and protect the interests of the individual over the demands of the task and of the organisation. Because these needs overlap, there is no necessary conflict between them, but there may well be tension. Shop stewards are elected leaders, accountable ultimately to the membership who elected them; supervisors, by contrast, are appointed leaders, accountable to those who have appointed them. There is no reason why both forms of leadership cannot live and work side by side. That prospect will be greatly enhanced if (1) as supervisor you take seriously your responsibility for developing, caring for and motivating each individual in your team, and (2) shop stewards take an intelligent interest in the progress and prospects of the business — which they will do better if you brief them with the necessary facts.

I can still remember my shock when, some years ago, Vic Feather, the General Secretary of the Trades Unions Congress, mentioned to me the annual figures of those badly injured or even killed at work. 'You see now,' he said to me, 'that what industry needs now is not bosses but leaders.' Chapter 8 takes up that theme. It reviews the supervisor's responsibility for health and safety at work. The best way of dealing with industrial accidents is to ensure that they never happen. It is your job to make certain that everyone has the appropriate training and that safety standards are rigidly adhered to.

No book can teach you how to be an effective supervisor. You have to learn by experience. But books such as this one can help you to cut down the time you take to learn from experience and to avoid the mistakes of others. Even the experienced supervisor will find here some useful benchmarks to measure his or her performance and development as an effective leader in one of the most challenging and interesting jobs in the world.

/YOU — THE EFFECTIVE SUPERVISOR

Chargehands, supervisors and foremen are by definition leaders, set apart from and above other employees. It is a strange position in which you find yourself: in your own time you socialise with your colleagues and share their interests and problems, but in company time you are expected to become their 'judge' and 'arbiter'. It can be difficult to come to terms with this double life, and in fact you probably find it very tempting to shelve your responsibilities for managing people and just muck in with the rest of the workers. However, of one thing you can be absolutely certain: if you do shed these leadership responsibilities you will never be able to manage in the true sense of the word — and nor will your workmates respect you for it.

Admittedly, as soon as you put on the white coat of office you are letting yourself in for a fairly tough ride. As a leader, you will find that much of your time is spent facing the music — dealing with complaints, suggestions, grievances and other enquiries. However, that is exactly why you are there: your employees have a right to complain and enquire, and it is your job to explain and justify to them any decisions which you might make. Should they still continue to carp and criticise, it is probably not you personally or your job that they are unhappy about: it is almost certainly the way in which you are managing your team.

What is a supervisor?

The Industrial Relations Code of Practice defines a supervisor as a 'member of the first line of management responsible for a work group to a higher level of management'.

Supervisors are part of their organisation's management team. They control the activities of others, and they have the responsibility of carrying out management's policies and intentions by leading the group that is in their charge. In short,

1

their task is to get things done through the correct management of the people for whom they are responsible.

It is not just because it is up to you to get things done that your job as a supervisor is an important one. To the members of your team you are the only member of management who really counts. The attitude of team members towards the organisation and the size of the contribution they are prepared to make to it depend very much on the way you do your job.

Perhaps because the job of supervisor is so important, a lot of people give the impression that it is downright impossible to do it properly. In fact it is not — as you presumably know very well. What the people who devise those impressive lists of necessary qualifications are ignoring is that

- people of all sorts of different personal qualities and abilities can and do make very successful supervisors
- every supervisory job is different from every other
- the same supervisory job can be successfully carried out in any of a number of quite different ways

The success of your organisation depends upon each supervisor — and his or her team — making a positive contribution. Often the pressures of work are such that your priorities will be primarily short-term productive ones. This is something you have to accept, but at the same time you must realize that your job as a whole covers not just the technical aspects — which are generally fairly obvious — but also the administrative and human aspects, which are all too often ignored by supervisors and, indeed, by their superiors.

So we can say that there are two main things required of you if you are to do your job properly. First, you must know what is expected of you — that is, what your particular functions are in your own particular organisation. Second, you must have an appreciation of the management of people, because without it you have not a hope of being a successful supervisor.

Of course, making sure that you are a good supervisor is not a matter only for yourself: management should give you every assistance. They should make sure that you have been properly selected and trained, that the work group assigned to you is of such a size that you can manage it effectively, that you are always fully briefed in advance about management's policies (at least insofar as they affect your work group), and that you are given the scope to be an effective communicative link between management and the members of your work group.

To put the supervisor's role and responsibilities into perspective, we need to look at the overall objective of management — which in its simplest terms is to deploy human and capital resources to create and satisfy markets in the most effective way. The efficiency with which this is being done can be measured by the profit which an organisation makes. Responsibilities at the various levels within an organisation may differ, but the common factor throughout all of them is the matter of profit.

'Profit' is often regarded as a dirty word, and it has to be admitted that the activities of some organisations have made it so. However, in general, industry and commerce, management and unions, workers and staff are all geared to the honest generation of material wealth. Virtually everyone wants a higher standard of living and more money in their pockets, but if this is to be achieved then the organisation for which they work must make a profit: whatever the arguments over how the profit is split up, no one will get anything unless there *is* a profit. After all, a small percentage of something is always going to be better than 100 per cent of nothing.

So your job as a supervisor is to help make your organisation more profitable: you have to achieve the objectives determined by higher management through the people for whom you are responsible. Your success, then, will be measured largely by your ability to get other people to work effectively. What can help you do this?

First, you must be in charge of a work group of no more than fifteen people — otherwise you will be unable to treat the group members as individuals and to delegate to them effectively. Next, if you are to enjoy the trust and confidence of your staff you must be able to tell them in advance about the policies or changes that will affect them. You must enjoy good working relations with the members of your group. You must take risks where necessary while at the same time being patient, and you must ensure that your group is well organised and that its members are appropriately trained to do their jobs. You must, as we saw in Chapter 1, ensure excellent communications with your subordinates, other supervisors and people higher up the management ladder. Finally, and most of all, you must accept the responsibilities of leadership.

Clearly you must have a thorough knowledge of the work which has to be done by your team, but it is just as important that you have a full knowledge of your own responsibilities. Your section and the people in it are not an isolated unit: they form part of a much larger team — the organisation as a whole — and so you need to have a good knowledge of the organisation, its aims and its standards. You are bound by the organisation's policies and so, if you are to be an effective leader, you need to be familiar with them. Here are some of the questions you must be able to answer:

- what is the main purpose of your company?
- what service does it provide, and to whom?
- what does your section contribute to this?
- is yours a public company and, if not, what type is it?
- what did your company's last balance sheet reveal?
- what are your staff's conditions of employment (holidays, overtime and so on)?
- what is the organisation's attitude to staff committees and joint consultation?
- what part do trade unions or staff associations play in the organisation's affairs?
- do you know your place — and your team's place — within the organisation?

This last question is especially important. It is vital that both you and your subordinates are fully aware of your section's relationship to the rest of your organisation — in other words, where you 'belong'. Too many supervisors are kept in the dark about such matters, and many more have even less idea about what their job entails. If you are in this position, bully senior management until they give you the necessary answers — and then make sure that you communicate those answers to your subordinates.

People

In his book *What Every Supervisor Should Know,* J. Bittel wrote:

No amount of policies and procedures, fancy cafeterias, generous fringe benefits, or sparkling toilets can take the place of supervisors who are interested in their people and treat them wisely and well.

The job of supervisors, as we have seen, is to get things done through the people beneath them. It follows that your effectiveness will largely depend on the way you treat other people. If you have a real respect for people — in other words, if you treat them the way you yourself would like to be treated — you will create the kind of atmosphere in which they will be able to give of their best. You will recognise that each individual has a contribution to make, and ensure that full use is made of the combined knowledge and experience of the people within the group. You will want the group to understand and as far as possible impose its own disciplines — self-imposed disciplines always being much more effective than any dictated from on high. You will not regard yourself as in any way a superior, but rather as a member of the group who just happens to have some special extra responsibilities. You are, in fact, the leader of a team and, like any team leader, you are utterly reliant on the other people in the team if together you are going to achieve the team's common aims as well as the aims which the organisation deems relevant to your jobs.

In this respect there are a few important things you must do. You must be accessible, not hidden away in an office. You should try to spend at least 70 per cent of your time out among your team, because otherwise you have no chance of knowing what they really think and feel. Walking the job (*see* Chapter 1) is as good a way as any for achieving this. Wherever possible, give the members of your team the opportunity to be responsible for taking decisions that directly affect their work situation — for example, so long as the section is staffed adequately throughout the holiday period, there is absolutely no reason why your subordinates should not work out the holiday rota among themselves, rather than having it imposed on them by you. That said, however much you delegate responsibility, the onus on you is that you must retain accountability: should anything go wrong it will be your fault, and you must be prepared to accept this. If you want the loyalty of your team you must keep them informed of any management decisions, proposals and future plans that might affect the team, and you must be prepared to explain the reasons behind such changes. Conversely, you must keep management informed of your team's reactions and requirements and, importantly, be seen to do so: your team members will soon stop telling you their feelings if they believe that no further action will be taken. Similarly, if anyone comes up with a good idea or suggestion or a useful criticism you should be seen to listen, evaluate and if necessary act. Finally, you should report to the team the progress it is making towards achieving its targets; you should recognise success, learn from failures, review objectives and involve the team members in planning or replanning for the future.

Some supervisors — bad supervisors — deride this sort of an approach as 'soft'. This is usually because they do not understand it or because they fear it will involve loss of their personal power. Do not fall into this trap. Granted, you may find that doing these things requires patience and perseverance — it is even possible that you might find yourself the lone voice for such an approach in management meetings — but it is nevertheless likely that the successes of your section will persuade the rest of management that your approach is right.

Just as with the management, it is possible that your subordinates will never before have encountered this sort of approach. People cannot be expected to take to it 'instinctively': they have to learn gradually and by experience. One of your skills is the ability to give the members of your team the right opportunity at the right time. If you are to do this you must

- set and maintain the group's objectives and standards and make sure that they are known and understood by every person involved
- involve the group as a team in the achievement of those objectives
- strive to make the group behave as a team, to minimise any discordance and to broadcast the achievements of your team
- gain the commitment of team members to implement management decisions, even if they disagree with them

Your dealings with individuals should, of course, be in the same spirit as your dealings with your team.

Leadership

As the person responsible and accountable for the activities of the members of your team, your aim must be to make full use of their strengths, skills, inventiveness and any other abilities they may have. If you are to get the best out of each subordinate, therefore, you have to develop your own ability to lead other people. In essence, your effectiveness as a leader depends on your ability to influence — and be influenced by — your teams and the individuals who make up those teams, so that all concerned can be involved in the carrying out of a common task. You have to ensure that the required tasks are completed satisfactorily while at the same time supervising your team so that teamwork and team identity are maintained and developed. At the same time, you must recognise that each person in the team is indeed an individual, who has needs, hopes, ideas and so on which must be realised if the individual is going to be effective, If you concentrate too much on achieving the task whatever the cost, then sooner or later your team will start to disintegrate; likewise, if you fail to recognise individual needs you will inevitably fail to spot the rotten apple, which means that soon you will have a rotten barrel and, once again, the team will disintegrate. If you are to be successful as a leader you must work in three main areas. These are:

- task needs
- team needs
- individual needs

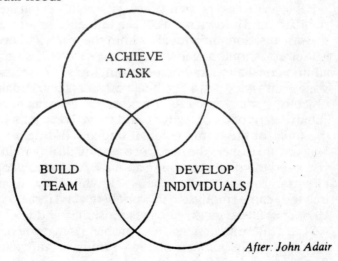

After: John Adair

As you can see, there is a tremendous overlap between each of these three interests — to choose a single example, individual needs will almost inevitably be best served if the overall team needs are being accomplished.

There are certain steps you can take to help you achieve the task while at the same time meeting the needs of the team as a whole and each of the individuals within it. In order to achieve the task you must have a clear idea of what it is, you must understand how the task fits in with the objectives of the organisation, you must plan how the task will be accomplished, you must define and provide the resources that you need (e.g., time, authority, staff and equipment), you must ensure that the organisational structure allows the task to be achieved effectively, you must control progress and you must evaluate the results.

A team has assets which, certainly in the working situation, can often exceed those of its members: the whole is greater than the sum of its parts. If you are to be an effective supervisor you must recognise the strengths, resources and weaknesses of your team. For example, while there are a greater number of ideas available on how to solve a problem, there is at the same time a greater potential for disagreement. On the 'plus' side, there is a broader base from which ideas and solutions can be sparked off, and there is a plethora of experience available.

Each team has its own power, its own personality, its own standards and its own needs. It can influence other teams within the organisation, individuals within the team, and even you, its leader. You should acknowledge these capabilities and take them all into consideration when deciding how you will act to meet your team's needs. In a nutshell, you must set and maintain team objectives and standards, involve the team as a unit in the achievement of its objectives, and strive constantly to maintain the unity of the team, marginalising any dissident activity.

If you are to meet the needs of the individuals within your team you need to know something about what makes people tick — in particular, what makes them tick while they are at work, so that they can be motivated to work better and more productively. Most of us like to work, enjoy responsibility and want to feel that we can achieve something. Your problem is that you have to make sure that the individuals in your team have sufficient scope so that they can satisfy these desires. A corollary of this is that you have to know why so many people habitually work less well than they could. There have been many surveys examining this latter

8

question, and their results can be summarised as follows:

- bad working conditions
- fear of redundancy, changes, inadequacy, and so on
- boredom
- personal worries
- poor supervision
- feeling of unimportance
- lack of incentive
- poor relationships with colleagues
- lack of information about the job and about the organisation as a whole.

To provide the right atmosphere and opportunities so that each of the individuals in your team can achieve job-satisfaction is probably the most difficult part of your job but, if you can do it successfully, it is almost certainly the most rewarding. Just a few examples of the things you can do are:

- help your subordinates to realise that work can be a satisfying and integral part of life
- provide clear targets by which their performance can be assessed
- consider any incentives — not necessarily financial
- give praise where praise is due
- keep people constantly informed of any changes, etc., so that they feel secure in their jobs
- respect your staff, and treat them as individual human beings
- involve your people in the overall job, so that they develop an interest in what they are doing
- keep a close eye on working conditions, notice any defects, and put forward publicly any recommendations you might have for improvements
- be constantly on the lookout for improved layouts, methods, systems and so on.

If you actively involve your team as a whole in determining objectives, in choosing working methods, in reorganising work schedules, in solving problems and in making decisions you will have your team behind you, backing you every inch of the way. You will be better able to change team practices than if you give separate instructions to each individual member or, even worse, simply impose new orders and instructions. If you involve the members of your team you will be better able to generate support for needed change, the implementation of new procedures, and so on.

Training for efficiency

If a job is to provide interest and challenge it must be constantly progressing and changing — which means that the person doing the job will often require training. You have certain responsibilities in the field of training — not just of new staff in specific skills but also of existing staff whose jobs are to be expanded or who you want to become more efficient and productive. Remember, if there is any gap between what you want a subordinate's performance to be and what that performance actually is, then it is your responsibility to ensure that the gap is closed through training. You are accountable for the job performance of all the people in your team, and so you must be ever aware of your responsibilities, of the essential functions of training, and of the methods whereby the training you arrange can be rendered more effective.

You have a twofold responsibility for the training of your people. First, it is your duty to develop deputies and train immediate subordinates, and to encourage them in turn to train theirs. Second, you must ensure that a comprehensive system of training them through you will find you are achieving greater efficiency in a number of areas: the organisation within your unit will be efficient and smooth, production will be of better quality and more economical, your staff will be individually more effective and will develop much better. Also, team and individual needs will be satisfied because your staff will have a sense of responsibility, their working relationships will be good, they will be cooperative and they will identify with the interests and objectives of the organisation as a whole.

Realising your responsibilities and actually doing something about them are two quite separate things. So, how can you go about training your people?

Essentially, there are four stages involved: assessing the needs for training, organising it, carrying it out and, afterwards, evaluating how effective it has been. To help you assess training needs you can draw up a plan showing who needs training and for what. You, as your people's direct supervisor, know better than anyone else the standard of personnel necessary if the job is to be properly done, the nature of the work being done and the skills required, and the size of the gap between your people's existing skills and those required. The organisation of training is largely up to you: even if your organisation has a training programme, you are the essential link between the training officer and your staff, and more often than not you will find that you are the person who has to carry out any on-the-job training — in which case you should prepare yourself thoroughly by examining people's job specifications and breakdowns and studying training manuals.

Means of carrying out training vary from on-the-job coaching to college or university courses, and similarly there are many training techniques — lectures, discussion groups, role-playing games, tape recorders, etc. — all of which have their pros and cons. However, most supervisors are concerned primarily with on-the-job training using demonstration and delegation — a subject to which we shall shortly return.

The final stage of training is evaluating how effective it has been. Your responsibility is to check how well the results of training have matched up to the original need. Also, of course, at this stage you have the opportunity to amend the future training programme in light of the effectiveness or otherwise of the current one.

Always remember that the trainee of today is the supervisor of tomorrow; if for no other reason, you have to be involved in the training of your subordinates. In his book *Psychology of Industry* Norman Maier remarked:

Regardless of how much training is done in a company before an employee reports to a particular supervisor, the supervisor must still do some training. Actually, giving work assignments, inspecting work assignments, inspecting and upgrading performance, should still be thought of as training.

The role of the representative

Your role, as part of the management team — and never forget that that is what you are, and certainly in the eyes of your people — is to maximise the resources at your disposal to the full limits of your authority. Indeed, it is precisely because you have the potential to do this that you have been made a supervisor.

11

Obviously, one of the most important resources you have available is the people of your team, but at this point the objectives of management can sometimes conflict with the desires of the employees. This is why staff elect representatives — in fact, they are doing roughly what management did when they made you a supervisor. Just as you are accountable to management, so employee representatives are accountable to the people who elected them; thus, when conflicts of opinion occur, the views of each side can be consistently represented in discussions and the problems can be resolved in the best interests of all concerned.

The representative's job is unpaid and not easy. Whether or not they have trade-union backing, they will have some good personal reason for wanting to take the job on: despite the claims of the popular press, in at most five per cent of elected representatives will this motive be a political one.

Whatever the title of representatives — "shop steward", "father of chapel", etc. — they have two roles: on the one hand, they are company employees, just the same as the people they represent, while, on the other, they have the responsibility democratically to represent the interests of the group of employees who elected them.

If you are the supervisor of a team which contains a staff representative you will obviously face something of a dilemma in terms of maximising your "people resource": from time to time the representative will be away from the job, having meetings with yourself or other members of the management team. This is something you have to accept: you need to acknowledge the fact that the representative has to have time off, and reorganise the work-patterns of the other people accordingly. You can make this much easier if you and the representative reach an agreement about the amount of prior notice he or she should give you before having to take the time off. Also, you and the representative may be able to agree on the amount of time he or she will need each week in order to carry out their representative duties, so that you can plan in advance how the workload is going to be coped with.

It is worth remembering that representatives should normally become involved in a problem only if it cannot be sorted out directly between you and the individual(s) concerned. Thus the way in which you tackle problems when they first come up has a tremendous influence on the involvement or otherwise of the representative.

The first loyalty of staff representatives, when meeting with you or other managers, is to their constituents. If the representatives are trade-union members, then they have further responsibilities — to their own union and to the trade-union movement as a whole. On no account should you expect them to have any responsibility for furthering the interests of management while they are handling issues on behalf of their members. Management is the job of managers; representatives are there to represent. They are out to achieve the best possible deal for their constituents: should they consistently fail to do this, the employees will replace them by someone better able to get good deals. It may well be that the representative personally disagrees with the policy he or she is promoting, but nevertheless it is their duty to pursue the interests of the majority of their constituents to the best of their ability. In this respect, positive action taken by you can help representatives accomplish their task in the best interests of both the organisation *and* the employees.

At all times you should recognise that representatives do a valuable job, and you should aim to develop constructive relations by meeting representatives as soon as they are elected (not waiting until the first problem arises), making it clear that you will work with and not against the representative to solve genuine problems, dealing swiftly with grievances or, if necessary, passing them further up the management ladder, and, finally, holding a regular short meeting with the representative for briefing and consultation, especially about change.

We shall return to the topic of employee representatives and industrial relations in general in Chapter Seven. Here, though, we can note that, unless you are very unlucky, the staff representative is potentially your greatest ally in getting your job done. If you start out by assuming that he or she is the foe, you are throwing away a major opportunity to improve your effectiveness as a leader.

Developing your staff

There are two main ways in which you can develop the individuals in your team: by delegation and by appraisal.

Most supervisors believe that they delegate, but rather fewer of them actually do. They get confused between delegation and allocation: if you simply allocate the humdrum parts of your work to other people, you are not delegating at all, because you are not giving those people any responsibility or authority, which is what delegation is all about. Obviously, yours must remain the ultimate responsibility, and you must retain the right of overall control, but the more your subordinates have their own responsibilities the better they will work for and with you.

There are many reasons why delegation is a good thing. For example, it gives you more time to think, to plan ahead and to do the supervisory part of your job. It develops the skills and potential of your subordinates, and is an essential part of the overall training process. It allows full use to be made of the staff's specialist skills, and staff will feel more involved with their job and derive more satisfaction from their work (and therefore do it better) if they are given responsibility.

Why are some supervisors so reluctant to delegate? There are a number of reasons, of which the selection below represents only a random sample.

- delegation involves individual people, which means that sometimes it can go disastrously wrong
- it needs planning and training
- some supervisors are afraid that their juniors are better able to do the job than they are themselves
- you think you can do the job better yourself (which may be true — but there may be more important jobs you should be doing instead)
- you may be loth to give up some of the detailed tasks which you enjoyed before you were promoted
- there are risks involved in delegation: sooner or later someone is bound to foul up
- the subordinate may not be genuinely willing — whatever he or she may say — to take on the responsibility, and so may come back to you for so many decisions that in the end you find yourself taking the job back
- unless you are absolutely clear as to what it is that you are delegating the subordinate will not really know what is expected and so may end up doing nothing — a situation you may not discover until some while later
- things go wrong because, having delegated a section of your work, you fail to let go of the strings and allow the subordinate to do it his or her own way, so that the resulting compromise satisfies nobody.

If you are to delegate successfully the first thing you must decide is what you can delegate. Here you must be harsh with yourself. Many supervisors think that every single part of the work that they do is uniformly important. So start by writing down a list of all the individual tasks you are currently performing and ask yourself for each of them: 'Why do I do this job?' In some cases your answer will be that no one else can do it, but often you will find that the honest answer is that it is part of your function only because it always been, because you enjoy doing it, or because management expects you to do it. Next, for each job, ask yourself: '*Must* I do it, and, if so, why?' In some cases your initial response will be that yes, you must do the job; but once you examine your reasons for saying that you will often find that in fact no, somebody else could do it just as well. So, assuming that you find there are a number of jobs you could usefully delegate, your next question to yourself should be: 'To whom?' It may be, of course, that none of your subordinates is as yet capable of doing the job, in which case there is a final question to ask yourself: 'Who should I be training?'

The actual process of delegation is much like that of training, and the principles are the same. Imagine you have a particular job which you want to delegate to one of your people. First you must convince the person that he or she really does want to take on the added responsibility by explaining why you want the job done and how it will help his or her career development. Next, you proceed to hand the job over in five easy stages.

First, you demonstrate how the job is done by doing it yourself, with the subordinate looking on. It is important even at this earliest stage that the subordinate should be encouraged to offer criticisms of the way you are going about the task. A fresh pair of eyes can often spot ways of doing the job more efficiently; and, if nothing else, the answer to the query 'why don't you do such-and-such?' will help your subordinate to avoid various pitfalls which might seem so glaringly obvious to you that you never think to mention them.

Once you have shown how the job is to be done, the second stage is to get the subordinate to do it while you look on. You should comprehensively brief the subordinate first, and of course you should allow for questions.

The third stage is to let the subordinate do the job without supervision. This should be preceded by further briefing, to make sure that the subordinate is quite clear about what he or she is supposed to do. While the person is doing the job, you should be available to answer any questions that may arise, and after the job has been done the person should report back to you as to whether or not he or she has succeeded in performing the task adequately.

Stage four is when you can let the subordinate do the job and simply report back to you on the outcome, and the final stage is when you can arrange that the subordinate simply receives the job straight from source — in other words, from where you used to get it. This is important: it makes it plain for all to see that you have handed over the responsibility and authority for doing the job to the subordinate. Obviously, you will still want to check from time to time that the job is being done well — after all, you are the person ultimately responsible for ensuring that it is.

At any stage up to the last, you are free to cease the delegation process if you realise that things are not going well. Indeed, you would hardly proceed to the fifth stage unless you were satisfied that the subordinate could do the job and take on the requisite responsibility and authority. Obviously it is better to hand a task over in this 'fail-safe' way than simply to throw it at someone in the hope that they can do it adequately — better for them, and better for you.

A last word on the subject of delegation. Delegation is a vital supervisory tool, but only if you *make* it work. You need to recognise the ability of your staff, you must have complete trust in them, you must have a genuine desire to develop them, and, finally, your delegation must be systematic.

The other major way of developing your staff is through appraisal. As we noted earlier in this chapter, it is important to set clear targets in order to improve efficiency; likewise, you should monitor performance on a day-to-day basis. However, it is also important to discuss with your subordinates their performance over a long period — say, six months or a year. Many companies do this with new staff but, once the 'probationary period' is over, let things slide — as if even experienced staff do not need to know how they are performing or, just as important, how they are being perceived to perform.

So, at least once a year, set aside a couple of hours or more for each individual in your team. Tell the person in advance that you want to discuss their work, and ask them to concentrate their thoughts in a few vital areas:

- is their original job description still valid, or has it been overtaken by events?
- what, if any, particular problems is the job throwing up?
- has the person any ideas about how these could be solved?
- is any specific help required from you?

The whole subject of appraisal and appraisal interviewing is discussed in more detail in a companion volume to this book, *The Action-centred Leader*. Here, though, we can note that the way you approach any appraisal interview is that it is a 'conversation with a purpose', and certainly not some kind of Star Chamber in which you will give your verdict on your subordinate's competence — and nor it is an opportunity for the individual to air his or her grievances. Make sure that your subordinate realises this beforehand — and make sure that you do, too.

Organising your own time

If there is one thing common to all supervisors it is their lack of time. If only they had the time to communicate, to train their staff, to delegate, to discuss personal problems with them ... Ah, how much better life would be. Instead of which, supervisors tend to do none of these things because they are too busy working.

How, then, do you find the time to do that important part of your job — supervising? One method is to organise your time so that you can establish your priorities and do the more important things in preference to the less important. You could write down the various elements of your job under such headings as 'Training', 'Checking completed work' and 'Liaising with other departments'. Then you can rearrange the listing so that each function appears in the order of its importance, and beside it you can put an estimate of the amount of your time it takes up each week. Looking at the list and at your estimates, you should ask yourself a few questions:

- are you spending enough time on the more important matters?
- can you reduce the time you are spending on the less important matters?
- what jobs might you be able to delegate?

- are all of the jobs still relevant, or could some of them be eliminated?
- have you any time left over for doing 'nothing in particular'?

Once you have your priorities worked out you should be able to establish a rough programme for your day-to-day activities. Some regular jobs must be done daily, some weekly, and some at longer intervals. A simple system is needed to make sure that none of them are overlooked. For example, you could keep a long wall calendar showing completion dates, appointments, special jobs to be done, and so on. Alternatively, you can keep a desk diary which performs the same function but allows room for more detail — although the calendar is obviously better for giving you a swift overview of your future commitments.

Whatever you decide upon, keep it simple, and make sure that its sole object is to allow you to organise your time more effectively. The better you organise your time, the more of it you will have in which to do all those important parts of your job which tend to remain undone because they are not urgent — like delegation, which takes up time in the short term but which in the longer term can ease your life considerably.

Time is money, as the cliché has it. To follow up the analogy, if you invest a few pounds now you will do the equivalent of winning the football pools sometime soon. Only, unlike the pools, your win is guaranteed!

A final checklist on leadership

- set the task of the team, put it across with enthusiasm, and remind people of it often
- practise the three circles (see page 7)
- plan the work, check its progress, design jobs or arrange work to encourage individuals or the team
- set individual targets after consulting
- at least once a year, coach each person to achieve progress
- delegate decisions to individuals: if not, consult those affected before you decide
- communicate the importance of each person's job
- support and explain decisions to help people apply them
- brief your team monthly on progress, policy, people and points for action

- train and develop people, especially those aged under 25
- gain support for the rules and procedures; set an example and 'have a go' at those who break them
- where unions are recognised, encourage joining, attendance at meetings, standing for office and speaking up for what each person believes is in the interest of the organisation and all who work in it
- serve people in the team and care for their well-being
- improve working conditions and safety
- work alongside people, deal with grievances promptly and attend social functions
- monitor action
- learn from successes and mistakes
- regularly walk round each person's place of work, observing, listening and praising

2 YOUR RESPONSIBILITY FOR COMMUNICATION

The success of supervisors depends, primarily, on their ability to communicate to all the people for whom they are responsible first what they need to do and second the importance of doing it. If you are to be a successful supervisor, you must also encourage communication in the opposite direction, so that you can harness the ideas, views and experiences of the people who are actually carrying out the job.

Why does communication matter?

Communication matters for a plethora of reasons.

First, communication failures are costly. For example, in one large organisation it was discovered that, out of thirty-five stoppages, no fewer than eighteen were due to failures in communication. The cost of these stoppages could not be measured merely in terms of the hours lost: they upset the whole rhythm of production, lessened cooperation between employees and their supervisors, and created ill-feeling, which always reduces productivity.

Second, during times of change within an organisation, the full benefits of the change can be achieved only where there is an adequate communication system for explaining directly, preferably face-to-face, to the employees what is required of them and why.

Third, adequate communication results in greater productivity, because employees direct their work more effectively and cooperate more with their leaders. One City organisation has actually monitored staff productivity and found that there is a significant upsurge after each monthly briefing by management or supervisors.

Fourth, you may find that people of good potential are leaving your organisation simply because they are unaware of their prospects. Finding and training someone from outwith the organisation is a costly matter, and it lowers morale among colleagues. In order to avoid such situations, you need to communicate to your subordinates what you think of them and what their futures within the organisation are likely to be.

Fifth, people will give of their best to their work only if they fully understand the decisions that affect them and the reasons behind those decisions. Your subordinates need to understand what they have to do and why, how they are performing against the budgets and the targets they have been set, and what their conditions of employment are. Given this understanding, they can become *involved* in what they are doing, so that you enjoy greater efficiency, higher morale, and improved cooperation.

Finally, would *you* be happy working if you did not know why you were doing your work? No, obviously not. So clearly you owe it to your staff to make sure that they are not in that situation.

What should I communicate?

The first thing to decide is: what are your priorities? The system of communication you use will depend on your answer to this question. Clearly you cannot tell everybody everything, or consult everybody about everything, because if you did you'd never get any work done.

The old idea was that you told your subordinates what you thought would interest them, skipping all the boring stuff. But this is not really good enough. If you operate this principle, you find that you are not only missing out many things which it is important that your subordinates understand, you are also telling them a lot of things which, while perhaps interesting, are of little relevance. Of course, it is more difficult to get across things to employees which they find essentially uninteresting, but nevertheless you should persevere, and make sure the points are fully understood.

This matter of *understanding* is important. It is the vital first step in ensuring that any consultations you have with your employees are successful. Too often, supervisors seek ideas and opinions in formal consultation structures without having first given their subordinates sufficient understanding of their work for realistic ideas and opinions to be generated. Moreover, people will go along with a decision with which they profoundly disagree just so long as they understand *why* it has been taken. If they do not, you are very likely to find yourself with a revolt on your hands.

The primary things that need to be communicated to people come under two headings: things that affect their job, and things that affect their employment. Under the first heading come all the things that will enable them to do their job better; under the second come all the things concerning their rewards for having done the job. It is vital — as much for the good of the organisation as for the good of the individual employee — that such matters be communicated effectively.

And doing so is an important part of your job.

Which method do I choose?

The worst communication method you can use is the grapevine. To be true, the grapevine can be useful, but you use it at your peril. Facts can be communicated accurately through the grapevine — and very swiftly: sometimes, for example, the news about a forthcoming appointment can be communicated before the formal decision has been made! The great disadvantage is that the grapevine always gives an *uncharitable* reason for any decision, and that is bad for employee cooperation. The grapevine will say that someone has been promoted because she is about to marry the boss's son, not because she is good at her job; and all the people who are not being promoted will feel (quite naturally) resentful. So you owe it to yourself, your organisation and your staff to make sure that there is some systematic way whereby they can learn about the things that matter.

There are three main ways in which you can communicate effectively:

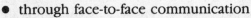

- through face-to-face communication
- through discussing matters with staff representatives
- through 'mass methods', such as a house journal or the notice-boards — although the former will probably be outside your control

You have to decide which method to use, and to be clear about what can be communicated through each of them and what the limitations of each of them are. All too often, communication breakdowns occur because managers and supervisors are using the wrong methods or because they are trying to communicate the wrong type of information through a particular system.

Face-to-face communication between supervisors and their subordinates is good in many ways. Part of the job of being a leader is to be the person to whom people look for explanations about the things that matter to them, and so, by becoming the direct communicator, you become a more effective leader. Moreover, you are in fact the best person to act as communicator, because you know — or should know — exactly why something is being done, and your subordinates will benefit from getting the news straight from the horse's mouth. You can tailor your explanation according to the interests of the particular group you are addressing, and then you can answer any questions that are forthcoming — something that is vital if your employees are to understand what is going on. Finally, face-to-face communication can save a lot of management time, ensures common understanding, and is the most powerful method of 'selling' ideas and building group commitment.

All of which might make you wonder why we bother even considering the other techniques of communication. However, the face-to-face approach has some weaknesses. For example, it can be very expensive in terms of the supervisor's time and, if there are more than two levels of communication between senior management and the front line, can be a total fiasco unless properly organised — which means that you or the management have to spend time and effort doing the organising. Another consequence of there being several levels of communication is that the hierarchy of leadership cannot by itself adequately cope with *upward* communication: senior management is often quite unaware of the vividness of attitudes at the bottom, because what has been reported to them has been diluted by passing through the various levels. Of course, you might think you are in an ideal position to prevent this happening, but however hard you try it is almost certain that, somewhere along the line, the attitudes of the workforce will be understated.

Communication *through representatives* has many advantages, because you can explain a policy directly to a few of the employees concerned, and discuss it with them; clearly this is more economical of your time and effort than setting up a system whereby policy is explained directly to every single employee. Also, representatives will tell you in forthright fashion exactly what the feelings are on the shop floor or in the typing pool; and the formal contacts made through meetings with representatives lead to more informal contacts, something which cannot help but be good for efficiency. However, although the representatives will usually understand your message completely, they will very often fail to pass it on accurately to those they represent — particularly in the case of unpleasant decisions. This is because the representatives are being put in the invidious position of being management mouthpieces: this is not their job, and if you force them to do it you are making both yourself and them look shoddy.

What, then, of *mass methods*? Notice-boards, house journals and so on offer the cheapest ways of giving information to large numbers of people, and they allow it to be done quickly. But, like the other techniques of communication, they have their problems. For example, while one of the strengths of a notice on the board is that you can ensure that the information you are transmitting is absolutely accurate, you have no way of knowing that it is being received accurately. Your employees cannot ask a notice-board a question, and so they may completely misunderstand what you are trying to communicate (a factor exacerbated by the grapevine). Likewise, although in theory people can ask questions at mass meetings, in practice most people are too shy to do so at any meeting where there are more than twenty present. Another important point is that mass means of communication can, by their very nature, cover only general aspects: what people *really* want to know is how they or their immediate working group are likely to be affected.

This matter of allowing for questions should be stressed. It is the only way in which you can ensure that everybody *understands* what is going on. There is a colossal difference between providing accurate information and getting people truly to understand that information. Experience has shown that, whatever other communication system you use, face-to-face encounters are vital, so that people can ask questions. Interestingly, explanation to a small group is better (as well as less time-consuming!) than to individuals: in a group, people benefit from hearing the answers to other people's questions and, of course, timid people profit through the fact that other people will ask the questions that they are too shy to ask.

Whatever technique of communication you choose for a specific situation, bear in mind that *any* systematic method is better than none at all. Obviously, the mass methods are easiest to use, and the face-to-face ones the most difficult. But, especially in a large organisation, communication both upward and downward will be unsuccessful unless you make judicious use of each of these three types of technique.

Effective communication through managers and supervisors

The busier your working life, the more important it is that you have mastered a systematic communication drill. You cannot afford to hope that communication will simply 'happen' in some kind of casual or *ad hoc* fashion. For example, you might explain some change with brilliant lucidity to your immediate subordinates but then, by the time the information has passed down to the other members of your team, find that the message has become utterly garbled. Even if it has not, what almost certainly *has* happened is that the people in the front line have concluded that the change will come about solely because 'they' have decided that it will, or that it was all a 'management decision'. You could hardly concoct a better way of ensuring that your subordinates are disgruntled.

Of course, because 'they' have ordained it, your team will almost certainly do what is required ... but they will not actively *cooperate*. And the difference between sullen obedience and constructive cooperation is very often the difference between loss and profit. If all you can get is obedience, then you are not doing your job properly.

If downward communication is to be effective then it has to be systematic. The object is to ensure that all employees have the decisions that affect their jobs or their conditions of employment fully spelled out to them, face-to-face, by their immediate boss. Two things are important if this is to come about: there must be a team-briefing drill that ensures communication, *via* supervisors, right down the line to the work group; and all the necessary information must be known to subordinate managers and supervisors.

Mass methods

Of all the mass methods of communication, the most noteworthy for the supervisor are the following: the notice-board, house journals, managers' newsletters, employee handbooks, loudspeaker systems, and mass meetings. Although some of these may be beyond your jurisdiction, let us look at each of them in turn.

First, *notice-boards*. The siting of these is important: not only should they be where people will see them, they should also be positioned such that people can actually stop to look at them. At each site there should either be two notice-boards or one notice-board overtly divided into two parts: one section can be used for new and/or urgent notices and the other for less urgent (but nevertheless important) matters. Once a notice has been in the 'urgent' section for forty-eight hours it should either be moved over, if it is important, or thrown away, if it is not. All notices on the board should be signed by an individual — otherwise the employees are likely to feel that they are part of nothing more than an impersonal web — and a particular individual (preferably the departmental supervisor) should be put in charge of each notice-board. A final point to note is that, when you are composing a notice for the board, you should think about how you would express the information were you actually *speaking* to the people, face-to-face. Write down what you would say rather than mess around with literary elegance. People respond far more readily if, as they read the message, they can 'hear your voice'.

The main purposes of *house journals* should be to provide a mass means of explaining the organisation's activities and policies to the employees, to help the employees feel that they are involved in the organisation, and to create an atmosphere in which change is accepted. The people responsible for budgeting and planning a house journal should be thinking in terms of frequency and flexibility. A gestetnered journal may not look like much, but it is far more topical than a glossy magazine that is always a couple of months out-of-date because of printing schedules.

The contents of a house journal should be regarded as being in three thirds: one third should be devoted to product and other news that affects employees' jobs; one third to developments or changes in conditions of employment; and one third to social events and ephemera. Of course, news that might affect jobs should already have been communicated, via managers and supervisors, to those directly concerned; but repetition here is useful to inform those who less directly concerned. The ephemera should not be regarded as an optional extra. One publishing company discovered that very few employees ever read its weekly newsletter until it began to contain joky reports of the antics of the company cricket team: suddenly everybody, whether interested in cricket or not, turned to the column hoping for a good joke, and ended up reading the rest of the newsletter. As a supervisor, you are well placed to contribute "fun" ephemera like this — better placed, in fact, than anyone in senior management.

Also, we can note here the *manager's or supervisor's newsletter*. This can be regarded as a company newsletter that applies to, and is distributed to, the employees of only a single part of the organisation; it is, of course, prepared by the relevant manager or supervisor. Such newsletters should appear at least monthly, and preferably more frequently than that: whenever there is something important to be communicated, an issue of the newsletter should appear — especially if there is any possibility that employees might misunderstand what is going on. And do not try to economise by running off too few copies: unless every employee has his or her own copy, the whole exercise is a waste of your time.

Each of your subordinates should have an *employee handbook* setting out the main rules and arrangements that apply to them. The handbook should be as brief as possible. If need be, it can be supplemented by booklets dealing with specific subjects — e.g., disputes procedures. The best way of presenting the information in employee handbooks is usually in question-and-answer form, explaining specific aspects of conditions of employment. For example, it may be obligatory to provide employees with the rules of the pension fund in their full legal rigour; however, the resulting document will be comprehensible only to a fully fledged lawyer, and so it makes a lot of sense to give employees a question-and-answer version, written without jargon, which they can actually understand.

Loudspeaker systems tend to be used too frequently. They are unsatisfactory for putting over a policy, as the listener often cannot even see the person speaking — let alone ask a question. So, unless you feel you really need it, drop the loudspeaker in a bucket of water at the earliest possible opportunity. Likewise, while *mass meetings* have a certain value, they are a poor means of ensuring that employees gain any understanding of what is going on because questions are impossible. Team briefing, working down the line, is a much more effective alternative.

Customer complaints

So far we have talked only about communication *within* the organisation. However, you may very well have to communicate regularly with people outside the organisation, and in no field can this be a thornier problem than that of customer complaints. Ideally, such complaints should be fielded by senior managers, but often enough you will find it is your turn to be buggins.

The most difficult situation in the field of customer relations is when something has gone wrong — the product has failed, promises have not been kept, deadlines have not been met ... Whatever the reason, the customer is quite rightly displeased, and it is up to you to deal with their displeasure.

It is quite understandable to want to go on the defensive — but it is also a big mistake. There is no surer way of losing a customer forever than to respond with something like: 'Well, no one's ever complained before.' You are implying that the customer is a pest and a fool, and, curious as it may seem, customers are not generally thrilled by this.

Oddly enough, it is actually more efficient to *encourage* customer complaints. They are a marvellous tool, providing more useful information about our products, services or performances than any number of surveys or praise-packed letters. If you use them correctly, complaints can work for you. Some researches have shown that companies which encourage complaints — for example, by having an accessible and publicized customer-relations or complaints department — can increase customer-retention by as much as 10 per cent. If you go one stage further, and are seen actually to do something about the complaints you receive — following them up and reporting back to the customer — your rate of customer-retention increases by a staggering 70 per cent. But if you pursue the complaints and come to a happy compromise.

By contrast, discouraging or rejecting complaints is bad policy. The same researches showed that, when customers found that their complaints were discouraged or that nothing was done about them, they told between 9 and 13 other people about the bad experience they had had; it is, after all, a natural human activity to gossip about the appalling treatment we have had at the hands of one company or another. This means that, by failing to communicate with customers who have complaints, you are not only losing those customers forever, you are ensuring that many potential clients would not touch your company or its products with a bargepole.

But there is more to it than that. Not only do dissatisfied customers tell the world about your organisation's shortcomings, they fail to tell *you* the reasons for their dissatisfaction. Unless you know why they are unhappy, you will never find out why it is that your organisation is losing customers — those customers who for one reason or another do not make a formal complaint, but simply cease trading with you.

It is therefore a vital aspect of communication to make sure that you listen to complaints and that you work to make sure that something is done about them. Of course, you may well be unlucky enough to be in an organisation in which the managers above you block all your best efforts to keep the customers satisfied. In this case, it is your duty to appeal as high up the management ladder as you can go. If you are still thwarted, you might consider looking for another job: organisations whose senior managers have no interest in customer satisfaction are unlikely to thrive.

Is communication working?

In these participative days, a key factor in effective leadership is the extent to which you pay serious attention to communication, both upward and downward. The more trouble you take over communication, the better your people will work for you and the better you will be able to work for those above you — not to mention the fact that all concerned will enjoy their jobs more. If you take action to improve communication, you will find that efficiency increases, 'as if by magic'. Except that there is no magic involved: all you have done is allow your subordinates and your superiors to get more out of their jobs — and hence more out of life.

As with all other aspects of leadership, it is necessary to check that your communication is actually working.

'Walking the job' is an effective technique. Every now and then (and it is worth booking the time in your diary, as otherwise the '*mañana*' factor comes into force!), simply walk around the place, chatting with the employees about their work, the weather, or anything else, and above all *listening* to what they have to say. You may be surprised by what you hear. If someone does not know why they are doing a particular job, or why a change has been made, then that means your communication system has broken down, somewhere along the line. For the short term, you should investigate the individual matter concerned, obviously; but for the longer term you should take a pretty close look at your own and your organisation's systems of communication.

Another, more formal, means of checking things out is through the use of questionnaires. There are two main types. In one, employees are simply asked how they heard about certain changes or decisions; their responses tell you how much you are communicating yourself and how much is being bruited about via the grapevine. The other useful type of questionnaire is the 'attitude survey', in which employees are asked — with guaranteed anonymity! — what they know about various organisational policies, what their attitudes are to the organisation and their bosses, what they think about their employment conditions, and so on. If you feel that such a survey would be of value, you might find it worth suggesting to your company's management that they employ an outside organisation to carry it out, as your subordinates may be reluctant to say what they really think if they feel there is a chance their remarks might be traced back to them. Both types of survey can supply you with invaluable information about communication failures, but be warned: you may not like a lot of what you discover.

The subject of communication is examined in much greater depth in my companion volume to this book, *The Communicative Leader*, from which this chapter has been adapted. Of course, there are many aspects of communication both within and outside your company over which you have no control — for example, you do not have the power to instigate a glossy monthly house journal — but nevertheless you should do everything you can to make sure that you are communicating management decisions effectively to your subordinates and that you are communicating upwards to management accurately, fully and forcefully. If your subordinates are unhappy about something and there is nothing you, yourself, can do about it, do not just shrug your shoulders and say: 'Well, that's the way it is.' Communicate the dissatisfaction up the ladder so that either (a) the problem is solved or (b) at least you get an explanation, so that you in turn can tell your subordinates exactly why the circumstance to which they object cannot be changed. Likewise, if one of your subordinates comes up with a good idea, make sure it is passed on upwards and that the person concerned is properly credited. (Some supervisors try to pretend that all the good ideas are their own. This is foolish. Their subordinates become bitterly unhappy — for obvious reasons. Remember, if one of your subordinates has a good idea you, too, will get kudos for having fostered that idea and for having had the sense to communicate it upwards.)

In this book we shall discuss various aspects of effective supervision. However, it cannot be stressed too strongly that, unless you make sure that you are communicating effectively, all of your other efforts are wasted. You may not *enjoy* communicating — you may be timid or you may simply dislike most of the people with whom you work — but nevertheless you must force yourself into the task ... and force yourself at least to *look* as if you are enjoying it — which usually means, after a while, that you find to your surprise that you actually are.

If you are a good communicator you improve the position of your own section of the organisation — in other words, of the organisation as a whole. You are therefore extremely likely to find yourself being promoted up the management ladder. It will then become your duty to pass your communication skills on to the supervisors working beneath you, as well as to deal with intra-organisational communications on a much broader scale.

Make sure, then, that you develop your communication skills now.

3 DISCIPLINE

Discipline is often regarded as a distasteful subject, because the habit has grown up of regarding discipline and punishment as one and the same thing. In fact, discipline in industry is better regarded as either (a) a system of rules for conduct or (b) a code of acceptable conduct. It is in these terms that we shall discuss the subject of discipline.

Disciplinary action — a much better term than the old idea of punishment — is of course necessary on occasion: it is usually the result of the breaking or breakdown of the code of conduct. You should never overlook disciplinary action, because it certainly has its place in the scheme of things. However, the prime objective of discipline is to try to ensure that this stage is never reached; or, should it come about, to make sure that justice is seen to be done and that the pre-existing code of conduct is reestablished. In doing the latter it is essential that you assess all of the causes of the breach of the code, and take any corrective action that is required: it may well be that the code is fundamentally unsound.

Essentially, there are two components of any company's code of conduct: accepted disciplines and imposed disciplines. The relationship between these two is of prime importance, and we shall return to it later; for the moment we can note that 'accepted' discipline refers to standards of behaviour, manners, etiquette and courtesy which are similar throughout most working groups. When we talk of 'imposed discipline' we are referring essentially to rules and regulations, legislation and other statutory requirements imposed by management.

The objectives of discipline

What does discipline set out to achieve? Well, it must further the ends of various different interests. For example:

- the organisation — this could include such matters as attendance, work rate, stability, profitability and public relations
- the customer — service, price, quality, delivery, value, presentation, etc.
- employees — safety, hygiene, welfare, security, wages, etc.
- the public — safety (especially in terms of the environment), social responsibility, company image, etc.
- the future — research effort, long-term security, use of people's creativity, etc.

These are only a few of the items that should be considered when management sets out to structure a disciplinary code within an organisation. Obviously, this does not mean that there should be a set of rules for every one of these items, simply that the effect of the overall code of conduct should be considered in terms of each of them.

This is the wider aspect of what discipline sets out to achieve, but a basic rule is that the general approach should be simple. If your team is helped to understand the overall objectives of the company, and if the individuals of the team know that success in achieving these objectives is a major factor in their future security and prosperity, you will never have to impose a code of conduct: the team members will derive it for themselves. This is what managing a more informed workforce is all about.

To be effective, any code of discipline must be seen to be fair, reasonable, logical and easy to understand, and it must be readily acceptable to the majority. If you are to achieve this, you must ensure that your people know not just what they are supposed to do but also *why*.

There are, of course, certain legal minima which must be included in contracts of employment to satisfy such legislation as the Health and Safety at Work Act (see Chapter Eight), the Employment Act and the Employment Protection (Consolidation) Act. However, whatever the company, its rules should be drawn up to suit the specific industry, product and environment. Briefly, we can list these under the following headings:

- protection and safety — of the person, the company and its resources, products, customers and shareholders
- creation and/or regulation of codes of behaviour in order to give parameters within which people can operate to their mutual satisfaction

- outlining minimum standards that will ensure the wellbeing of the organisation and its employees
- prevention of inefficiency or losses
- public relations, showing that the organisation is of good standing in the community

To achieve all these things it is not necessary that the organisation publish a vast book of rules — but it is necessary that all personnel, including the members of your team, should understand the organisation's overall objectives. In other words, good communication, proper and maintained training and good relationships between the various levels of the organisation are all prerequisites to good discipline. Legislation imposed from above but without any general commitment is, as we have seen over the past few years, definitely not the key to better behaviour. By contrast, a workforce which is better informed and which is united in its ambition to achieve its objectives usually gives rise to a successful organisation. So, make sure you know what your own objectives actually are, and then communicate them to the other members of your team.

Effective discipline

As we have seen, there are two types of discipline: accepted and imposed. The first represents codes of good behaviour, the second rules and regulations. Infringement of either type of discipline involves penalties. People who break accepted codes of behaviour can be 'sent to Coventry', all cooperation outside the requisite minimum may be withdrawn from them, or, as one supervisor once put it, they may be 'roasted on the gridiron of public opinion'. People who break imposed rules may, in extreme cases, find themselves in prison.

These penalties are severe, and largely unjust. To use an analogy, a person convicted of reckless driving — and who may have thereby endangered human lives — is likely to be regarded less as a villain by his or her colleagues than as some kind of a daredevil hero. On the other hand, someone who simply has a rude manner or who is believed to be a management 'sneak' can be put under such pressure by their colleagues that they have little option but to leave the organisation.

There are occasions when the two forms of discipline are clearly

34

in accord, when both colleagues and 'the law' agree that a person has been guilty of some kind of misconduct. When accepted discipline and imposed discipline are in agreement, it is obvious that the imposed rule is reasonable — that is, it is reasonable to the majority of the workforce. If it is not, it is probable that breaking the rule will become an accepted practice. A rule that is considered unreasonable by large sections of the workforce may not in fact be so: what has happened is that it has not been understood and is generally perceived as being gratuitously restrictive.

For example, rules against smoking on an oil platform are accepted, understood and often policed by the majority. However, in a foundry, a no-smoking rule might be widely considered unreasonable. It may well be that there is a reason for such a rule, but unless everyone knows that reason the rule is likely to be widely broken and may indeed become a topic of industrial discord.

The importance of having rules understood can be realised if we take a real-life example. A young apprentice in one company was told not to use the grinding wheel on brass and copper laminate. He was given no reason for this instruction and, as he thought he had discovered a way of working more quickly and thereby increasing his bonus payments, he assumed that it was merely a question of the foreman wilfully imposing restraints. So, as soon as the foreman's back was turned, the apprentice used the grinding wheel on some brass and copper laminates. Soon after he had finished, a fitter used the same grinding wheel to sharpen a large high-speed drill: within seconds the wheel jammed on the drill and shattered, with the result that the fitter lost an eye. The apprentice was not unnaturally distraught: as he wept he was heard to say, 'If only he had told me why!' The apprentice was quite right: he should have been told why. Even the most obvious of rules should be explained, and if they are in any way complicated they *must* be.

The best imposed disciplinary rules are acceptable to the majority. Some would say that, if the rules are so widely acceptable, it seems unnecessary to impose them at all; but imposed rules are usually designed not for the majority but for the minority, and it is necessary to have some basis of conduct, if only so that standards and procedures can be built upon it. At the very least, a set of agreed procedures should be in existence.

Another consideration when we think about the rules is the

nature of the rule book. Most organisations have some kind of rule book, but great problems can be created sheerly because of the length of these documents. If they are too long, no one ever bothers to read them, and all too often rules remain in the book for years after they have lost any relevance. Added to the old and obsolete rules is the annual crop of new rules brought into being because of, for example, changing technology. Many of these new rules may be very necessary, but they are likely to be lost in the plethora of unnecessary and/or out-of-date ones.

A good example of the kind of nonsense failure to review the rules can create occurred a decade or so ago in one very large organisation. A mediator had to be called in because many of the workforce had gone on strike after a person had been suspended for smoking in a no-smoking area. The manager responsible for the suspension was new, and had been specifically instructed to tighten up what seemed to be slack discipline in the section. The particular 'offence' had taken place outside, in an open space, directly under a very large NO SMOKING sign. Two previous offenders had been severely warned for smoking there.

At the mediation meeting attended by the individual, his representatives, the manager and the director, the first question the mediator asked was: 'Why is that particular area designated a no-smoking area?' This was probably the last question anybody had expected, and no one could immediately reply. The meeting was adjourned, with the workers agreeing to return to their duties while enquiries were made.

A couple of days later the mediator was telephoned to be told that all was well: the individual concerned had been reinstated, and the strike was over. The mediator repeated his question and, after an embarrassed pause, heard: 'Well, in 1942 we used to store high-octane fuel at that spot, so the sign was put up.' 'When did you stop storing it there?' asked the mediator. 'Ah — well,' came the reply: 'In 1944, actually.' So for more than thirty years the sign had been in place — moreover, being repainted regularly! — and nobody had thought to question the reason for this rule.

Subsequently that organisation went through its rule book and discovered that its length could be reduced by more than 75 per cent. The organisation's industrial discord was, obviously, reduced by an even greater figure.

So the short recipe for effective discipline is this: make it objective, reasonable and easy to understand, and involve everybody concerned with its structure and maintenance — at

36

the same time as you avoid everything that will be almost certainly unacceptable to the majority and ineffective in practice.

Rules and regulations

Acceptable rules and regulations are necessary if only to legislate for that minority who seem incapable of working in accordance with any normal code of behaviour.

Words like 'involvement' and 'participation' have been buzzwords for a number of years. Commitment of the workforce to the organisation's objectives is by now a long-established method of getting maximum effort. If people from all levels of the workforce are involved and participate in the construction of a system of rules and regulations you can expect maximum commitment, which is a good first step towards acceptance and understanding of the system. On the rules committee there should be representatives from front-line management, the unions (if they exist), and the training department; a representative from the personnel department should act as either chairperson or secretary. (A similarly structured group should be involved in regular revisions of the rules.)

What rules and regulations are necessary? For any organisation, there are two basic types. First there are the common rules required by law: these include contracts of employment and the conditions prescribed by the Health and Safety at Work Act and its attendant regulations as well as legislation concerned with industrial relations and employment protection. Some organisations find it useful to publish these rules separately since, because they are the law of the land, there is nothing much about them to debate.

Second, there are the rules which apply specifically to your organisation. The committee whose job it is to devise or revise the rules should, from the outset, have a clear understanding of the objectives towards which the rules are to be directed. This done, it should not take long before a basic skeleton is constructed, upon which the committee can then proceed to put flesh. Normally it takes four or five meetings to define the necessary basics, which can then be edited into a logical set of notes which become the basis of the rule book.

The most successful rule books state, immediately after each rule, the objective of that rule, and also include recommendations for acceptable behaviour — i.e., things that are not necessarily rules. Successful rule books are also as short as possible. A rule book that has both of these qualities is that of a well known food-processing company. It is fourteen pages long, and seven of those pages are devoted to explaining the objectives of the rules — in other words, what they are there to achieve. One page is taken up by an agreed statement made jointly by the unions and management giving their commitment to both the rules and the objectives, and there is another page devoted to disciplinary and appeals procedures. Since there is also a page left blank for notes, this means that all the rules are contained within a mere four pages — of a book that measures only five inches by three inches! This rule book has been in operation for many years, and as yet no problems have been encountered.

Studying parliamentary legislation can give us a lot of lessons about how to establish company rules. Most of them are 'don'ts':

- don't make excessive rules — think carefully if five or six separate items could be covered by a single short rule
- don't try to cover every aspect of interpretation by double-dotting every 'i' and double-crossing every 't' — this usually leads only to more confusion and more loopholes
- don't incorporate marginal rules or rules whose only reason for existence is that they cover up shortcomings

On the positive side, remember that the people covered by the rules or expected to adhere to them should always be involved in drawing them up, that brevity and clarity are essential so that every member of the workforce is sure to understand the rules, and that above all you should use common sense and logic in drawing up the rules — if some of the 'laws' are an ass then people will inevitably disobey all of them.

Even if you have not been involved in compiling the rules, you may very well find yourself required to help in the next stage: 'selling' the rules. In fact, there is no reason why the people who formed the original committee should not do the training of both yourself and your team: after all, they can answer any questions that arise, and should — certainly should — be able to explain the reasoning behind any particular rule. Management and unions together should be involved in implementing and applying rules, as it is always a good thing for these two influential bodies to be seen working in concert, and simply talking over the points on which they generally agree can help them to come to a good compromise on those points on which they initially disagree. Overall, if carried out in a calm and logical manner, the formulation and publication of a good rule book outlining discipline and disciplinary procedures can be a very constructive and worthwhile exercise, benefiting not just the organisation as a whole but also every employee within it. However, this can only come about if you — and all the other supervisors — are committed to the new rules; after all, you are the people who will have to maintain discipline according to the rule book. So you should be involved in the drawing up of the rules. If management shows no signs of involving you in this way, ask why not. Do not be afraid of asking pretty loudly!

Disciplinary actions

After you have drawn up a set of rules, trained everybody, ensured organisation-wide understanding and with the best will in the world done all the right things, what do you do if someone flagrantly disregards a rule? Obviously, you must think about disciplinary action. Before we discuss the details of this, it is worth first asking a question: what do you want the disciplinary action to achieve?

The answers given by supervisors, managers and even the workforce cover a wide spectrum: to punish, to set an example, to discourage repetition, to expose the person's malfeasance publicly ... What you should really be trying to do is to get the person's cooperation and bring him or her back to an acceptable standard. This may sound trite, but in fact all you want from any employee is that he or she works to an acceptable standard. A breach of the disciplinary code obviously means that the person involved is, at least in part, not according to the proper standard of performance. If the person's performance is otherwise all right, then your real objective is to amend the offending aspect, not to be some kind of Judge Jeffreys.

Also, it may just be possible that what is at fault is not the person but the rules. A leading publishing company used to have a rule that all its executives should appear for work in suits. Then a designer and an editor both started to turn up for work in jeans and denim jackets. When asked why, they pointed out that they worked better in casual clothing, and that surely the quality of their work was much more important than their sartorial elegance. The company reconsidered its policy, cancelled the rule, and enjoyed increased profits as most of the rest of the staff showed that they, too, worked better in comfortable clothing.

Sometimes disciplinary action is necessary as a sort of *aide memoire;* occasionally, to stay with French, you may need to use it *pour encourager les autres* — although in this case you run a very good chance of being unfair to the individual. We shall discuss the various disciplinary actions in terms of the objective we have stated above: the return of the individual to an acceptable standard of performance.

For the most part, people who break the rules do so only occasionally or through simple fecklessness. There are, however, a few 'hard cases' who can be dealt with in only one way: dismissal. This is the ultimate sanction, and should be used only as a last resort, after several warnings, or in the case of one of the few offences where, for safety reasons, no second chance can be given — smoking in a refinery or a coal mine, theft, physical assault, and so on. The decision to dismiss someone should never be taken lightly, and nor should it be taken unless you have made the fullest enquiries as to the reason for the breach of the rules; likewise, you must ensure that you are not creating a precedent, and that similar offenders have not been treated more leniently. You should certainly make sure that the employee's representative is involved in the procedure, as otherwise you are very likely to be involved in further problems — quite possibly legal ones.

It is worth repeating that dismissal should be very much the last resort. Aside from anything else, the fact that you have to dismiss someone may well be a sign that you are not being as effective a supervisor — i.e, a leader — as you should be. It is rather harsh if someone should lose their job because of your managerial failure.

A sort of half-way house is suspension, which is still in common use, although in some instances — especially if it is suspension without pay — it is against the law. If, however, there is an agreement in the contract of employment that suspension can be used then you are free to use it. However, there are a number of reasons why it is a bad idea:

● you may need that person's services suddenly: being only human, they are hardly likely to be wildly cooperative if you 'phone them up in desperation

- you may need that person's services in the long term, and find that, being suspended, they find alternative employment
- even after reinstatement, the person may have been so demotivated by the experience of suspension that they act as nothing more than an irritant to the rest of your team

Suspension with pay, by contrast — especially if it is pending enquiries or if it has to do with the individual's well-being or safety (as where someone is incompetent at their current task, but might be trainable for another) — is usually understood by and acceptable to the individual and to the workforce as a whole.

'Black marks' and written warnings are in common use and, if employed correctly, can be constructive; if used carelessly, though, this type of disciplinary action can have a very bad effect. Any form of warning you give must be preceded by a full discussion so that the employee properly understands the situation, and you must agree on a certain period after which the 'black mark' or warning will be removed from the person's record. If the person understands that the situation can be retrieved by good behaviour in future such warnings can have a constructive effect. Obviously, written warnings or 'black marks' should be issued only after at least one informal warning.

Transfer is another common disciplinary action: usually it means not just a change of job but a change to one of lesser status. All too often, managers and supervisors fail to think sufficiently about what they are doing before transferring someone for disciplinary reasons. If you are not careful, all you are doing is passing the buck — you are putting a disgruntled employee into someone else's team — and, even if the employee accepts the situation with reasonable grace, he or she may not be welcomed in the new team. Transfer can be very traumatic for the individual, and may lead to them quitting the organisation. On the other hand, if it is made clear that they are moving a square peg from a round hole to a square one, the action is not only justified but can also be of great benefit to the individual and indeed to the organisation as a whole.

Demotion is sometimes used as a disciplinary action, but it is a dangerous thing to do. Even if it is used in order to obviate what would otherwise be a redundancy, the individual concerned is hardly likely to be highly motivated. On occasion, demotion can be coupled with transfer, so at least the person is able to save face, but generally it is kinder to dismiss than demote. Sometimes, however, demotion can meet the needs of both the individual and the organisation — as when a person is old, cannot cope with their current job, and wants something less stressful — which they may be able tackle very satisfactorily. A thing to avoid is the sideways move to a non-job: everyone, not least the person concerned, knows what this means.

Fines are used in some companies, but often they are illegal. Not paying someone for time lost because they have been habitually late for work or because they are underproducing is acceptable, as is holding back increments provided there is no legal obligation to give them. Likewise, giving no or only a minimal increase as a result of a performance review is acceptable as a sort of fine. All of these sanctions should, like a 'black mark', have a fixed time period so that the individual can improve his or her performance, and you should be prepared to offer help if that is what the individual really needs. On top of everything else, any sort of financially punitive system should be fully understood by the individual concerned: otherwise you will simply be creating for yourself a situation where one of your team is being financially penalised, does not know why, and is quite justifiably making ugly remarks about your quality of management.

There are many other possible ways in which you can take disciplinary action. However, the overall rule is that, the less often you have to take action, the better a supervisor you are.

Disciplinary and grievance interviews

Any disciplinary action should be preceded by a discipline or grievance interview, a face-to-face and frank exchange of views. Even should the individual have been caught red-handed in the most heinous of crimes, it is still important for you to find out why: what was the root cause, the objective and the logic (if any) behind the action? The discipline interview can be the single most important part of the whole disciplinary procedure, but to be effective it must be carried out well and structured very carefully.

Clearly there are differences between disciplinary interviews and grievance interviews, but the basic rules are the same. You should remember that a successful grievance interview, which results in the obviation of a grievance, may thereby mean that you do not find yourself later performing a disciplinary interview with the same person.

For a disciplinary interview you should first remember the purpose of the meeting: you are there to inform, to correct mistakes or bad behaviour and to try to prevent such things happening again, to establish understanding of the required standard and to bring the person back to this standard. Before the interview, you must prepare yourself in several ways. You must gather the facts (consulting with others, reviewing the person's previous record, etc.), plan your approach in terms of the character of the individual involved, ensure that the meeting can be carried out in private, without interruptions, and that there is sufficient time for it, notify the person of the purpose of the interview, and so on. You should also notify other people that the person will be absent from his or her job for an hour or two. One important thing to watch is that you should not prejudge the issue: make sure that you do not enter the interview assuming that the person concerned is automatically guilty.

In the interview itself your first task is to put the person at ease, as in any interview. At all times you should keep calm, avoiding shouting and bad language. You should tell the person what the perceived offence is, and then allow them to state their case — and *listen* to what they have to say. It is quite likely, in fact, that you will have to help the person state their case by asking open-ended questions — what, when, where, how and who. Once you have established the cause of the problem, you should be constructive in showing how improvements can take place and, if possible, get the person to suggest how those improvements can be made. Finally you should ensure that both of you clearly understand the standards that are required of the person and state the action that is to be taken by both parties.

The final stage is what you do after the interview. Clearly you have to record what went on during it — otherwise you may find yourself with trouble on your hands. Also you must check on the individual's further behaviour, performance and attitude. You must check that the individual is given any help that might be necessary, and praise any improvements in his or her performance. Always remember that your objective is to return this person to an acceptable standard of performance, and ensure that the person understands this and understands what the acceptable standard of performance actually is. Although you must be aware of the sanctions you can take, the most vital aspect is that the interviewee should understand their own failing and themselves act to correct it.

A grievance interview is rather different. Its purposes are to allow individuals to air their own grievance(s) and to discover and if possible obviate the cause of their dissatisfaction. To prepare for such an interview you have to try to establish the circumstances which are giving rise to the individual's dissatisfaction, check with colleagues and with the person's record in case he or she is simply a habitual grouser, check with company policy so that you know what you can and cannot do, and ensure that you have enough privacy, time and so on. As with a disciplinary interview you need to put the person at ease, state the purpose of the meeting, and then allow the person to say what the grievance actually is. You have to establish not just the facts — which may be peripheral to the grievance — but also the feelings of the person concerned. Obviously, you should listen attentively, and you should avoid evading or belittling the issue — nothing will alienate the employee more than the impression that you do not take the matter seriously. You must probe in depth to ensure that you exract all the relevant facts, but at the same time you must not be too eager to commit the organisation to a particular means of solving the person's problem. If there is an obvious course of action, then state it, but, if there is not, at least tell the person roughly what you plan to do. Most important, try to get the person to suggest ways in which their problem could be solved.

Following up is as important for a grievance interview as it is for a disciplinary one. If necessary, investigate the facts, decide what should be done on the basis of your investigation and communicate your decision to the person involved, check that the results are the ones you want, and make sure that you have a brief informal meeting with the person later. You can learn a lot from grievance interviews, but beware of the 'professional moaner'.

During a disciplinary interview the employee's representative is entitled to be present; however, it is often more constructive if the initial interview is held on a one-to-one basis. Employees should be told of their rights, obviously, but they should also be told that a one-to-one interview is likely to be more effective in obtaining a better understanding. If the person insists on having a representative present then you, too, should have a back-up.

Certainly at the stage of a first or verbal warning you should try to keep the interview as informal as possible; even if you are at the stage of a final warning you may be able to keep the meeting reasonably informal. As with any other interview, if both parties are tensed up it is likely that nothing useful will come out of it; conversely, if you try to make the interview a friendly one you may reap great benefits. For example, one organisation discovered that a person being subjected to a disciplinary interview had considerable talent: he soon became the works manager. At the interview he remarked: 'That's the first time anybody has ever listened and agreed to help.' The lesson to be learned is that, if a person's creativity and talent are not fully harnessed for the use of the organisation, they may still be used — against the organisation.

Causes of breaches of discipline

In a survey carried out some years ago it was discovered that the causes of breaches of discipline could be grouped into three categories: 75 per cent were due to frustration, 20 per cent arose because people were seeking personal gain (in every sense of the word), and the remaining 5 per cent were 'miscellaneous'. In any one year, about 4 per cent of an organisation's employees were likely to be involved in some kind of disciplinary action. As three-quarters of these cases were the product of frustration, some further study was done to track the events leading up to the frustration, and in most cases a definite pattern emerged: initially there was some kind of misunderstanding; then there was a simple problem or complaint which was not dealt with, so the employee began to resent the situation; then there was a genuine grievance which was not dealt with, leading to either aggression or regression on the part of the employee; the employee's manifest dissatisfaction was not tackled, leading the person to depression and in turn to a frustration which was not dealt with, so that the final result was stark apathy. A majority of people who had valid questions to ask, it was found, were not discussing them with their supervisors but with their colleagues; often the result of their discussion with their colleagues was the wrong answer. If the people did feel that their problem was important enough that they had to discuss it with their boss, the typical responses they received were:

- Does it have to be now? I'm very busy.
- See the wages people. It's their problem.
- The personnel department can sort that out.
- That's not your problem — don't worry about it.

All of these responses — and many others like them — lead employees to feel justified grievance and to have a 'couldn't care less' attitude; they are the symptoms of a supervisor who is either overworked or just plain irresponsible. Whatever the case, you must always remember that what to you seems a minor worry is, to the individual involved, fairly major — otherwise he or she would not have come to you about it. You have to deal with the complaint as quickly as possible: often just the fact that you are prepared to listen to it will make the person feel better and so resolve the problem. If the problem remains unresolved you are likely to find that yet another person leaves your staff or that you are being forced to indulge in disciplinary interviews.

One frequent complaint of supervisors is that they have insufficient authority. If you feel like this, it may be that you are giving your authority away by passing on every problem to more senior or specialist management. In this case, adherence to a set procedure is paramount: you, as the person's immediate boss, must be the person who deals with any individual problem that comes up, passing it on only if it really cannot be solved at your level.

Obviously, the best way to deal with disciplinary problems is to make sure they never happen in the first place. How do you go about this?

Human beings do not have a particularly strong sense of instinct, but experienced and knowledgeable supervisors develop a 'sixth sense' that warns them of any impending crisis. Such supervisors have thought about the personalities of the different individuals in their team, and usually have a good relationship with the workers' representative; they always find time to 'walk the job', and they do not allow the pressures of work to bog them down in the office. Generally speaking, they are good delegators and effective motivators, and are well liked by the workforce. All told, they generate a happy atmosphere among the workforce, so that disciplinary problems are unlikely to arise.

The other thing you can do is to *anticipate* problems. No amount of rules, regulations, established procedures and so on will ever substitute for the straightforward application of common sense. Thanks to the pressures of modern working life, the 'urgent' often takes priority over the merely 'important', which means that in due course the 'important' crops up as 'urgent' because the matter has got out of control. A systematic way of tackling your priorities, coupled with good anticipation of likely difficulties and the ability to screen out all the redundant information that comes your way, will help you to avoid crises. Most important in the field of discipline is that you encourage your people and their representatives to discuss their problems with you as soon as they arise: you must always be prepared to listen and to act.

In discipline, as in most other areas of your job, prevention is the best cure.

Induction

We shall come back to the whole subject of induction later, in Chapter Five, but it is worth looking at it briefly here in terms of disciplinary matters.

New employees, whether this is their first job or their ninetieth, have three basic worries:

- will I be able to cope?
- will 'they' like me?
- will I fit in?

Starting any new job is fairly traumatic for anyone, and when one is worried about insecurities like these it is not the best time to be landed with extensive and possibly incomprehensible lists of dos and don'ts. Those aspects of first-day induction concerning discipline should be kept to an absolute minimum. Of course, you have to include items concerned with safety, timekeeping and the basics of the ladder of responsibility, but otherwise keep it simple. After the first week, when the new employee is more settled, you can start to give the disciplinary information that requires more concentration on their part, and provide a more detailed account of the organisation.

In too many organisations, newcomers find that sets of books and manuals, including the rule book, are simply dumped on them on their first day with the peremptory instruction: 'Read this.' It is doubtful whether one in a hundred ever do, and it is unlikely that even the people who obey the command actually understand the rules or their underlying reasons. The chances are better after the newcomer has been working in the organisation for a week or two, but then it becomes even more important to explain the rules, so that their reasons can be discussed and any questions answered. The obvious person to discuss disciplinary matters at this stage is you, the new employee's direct boss: after all, you will be the individual immediately responsible for the employee's conduct. Moreover, if you are the person who explains things to the new employee, you will establish your authority right from the outset, and will also give the employee a chance to relate to you in the right way. If you carry out the induction interview sensitively, you will induce in the employee an early understanding and a wish to cooperate with you.

Good induction is very important in establishing in the new employee's mind the correct code of conduct, and is likely to obviate any possible difficulties in the future. So do not leave the matter to chance.

Discipline and leadership

One way to raise the morale of people at work — and therefore their standard of behaviour — is to be a good and effective leader. This means that you have to assure yourself of the support both of your team as a whole and of all the individuals in it.

Effective leadership will in itself create a cooperative atmosphere in the team, so that discipline will be very much a matter of self-discipline, the team and its individuals doing your job for you by monitoring their own standards. Part of your task as a leader is to ensure that communication is good (see Chapter One) and that your workers thoroughly understand both their objectives and the contribution they can make to the achievement of those objectives. Further, by involving the team as a whole and the individuals within it in the allocation of tasks, you can get a high level of commitment from them, which again is likely to contribute to good discipline and a high level of performance.

If you are an effective leader you will respect the people in your team, and they will respect you. People who respect their leader are much less likely to act against the organisation than people who work in an environment where the leader is seen as someone who simply dishes out work and imposes discipline. As has often been noted, if the team is of a reasonable size and if the leader is given sufficient authority, breaches of discipline are few and far between.

A good leader is an *accepted* leader, and will always be prepared to listen to, help and advise the members of his or her team. Individuals will receive reassurance, and the leader will publicly demonstrate enthusiasm for their ideas. If you act in accordance with these principles, the chances are that none of your team-members will breach discipline, and indeed they will support you and produce work to the best of their ability. Good leadership is, therefore, a prerequisite to good discipline. If you are not prepared to make yourself into a good leader, then you can expect a troubled time on the disciplinary front.

4 ABSENTEEISM

There are two reasons why employees stay away from work: either they have to — because they are ill or otherwise incapacitated — or they choose to. In both cases, it is part of your job to discover why the absentee is absent and to get him or her back to work at the first possible opportunity.

In this chapter we shall consider the forms and causes of absenteeism and the factors that affect it. Clearly, the problem of absenteeism concerns you on two fronts. First, there is the overall problem of absenteeism within your organisation, about which there may be little you can do, unless you have a bright idea which you can pass up the management ladder via, for example, a suggestion scheme. More local to your work is absenteeism within your own team, and clearly there is a lot you can about this. The most important thing is to motivate your people, so that they want to work — a recurring theme in this book.

Some definitions and measurements

Before considering or implementing any policy to control absenteeism, management should ask itself how much absence there actually is, how much it costs, what forms it takes and how many employees are involved. Absenteeism means different things to different organisations, and there are a number of different ways of assessing the scale of the problem. For example, for a minimum figure you could consider only wilful absence for which there is no excuse; to this you could add sanctioned or unsanctioned absence for which there is an excuse; to these causes you could add medical incapacity, whether certified or not, plus annual holidays, jury service and even company-sponsored training courses. The International Labour Organisation and most experts in the UK suggest that it is a mistake to include absence through holidays, jury service and training in your calculations.

Also, the units you choose for measuring the rate of absenteeism have a profound effect on your calculations. Four units are in common use: hours (sometimes calculated to the nearest minute), working shifts, the National Insurance six-day week, and calendar days. In fact, it is a good idea to use more than one of these ways of measuring absence levels: you want to be able to assess both the duration of the absences (severity) and the number of absences (frequency), because a lot of short absences can have a worse effect than a few long ones.

For example, a civil craftsman's shop had a total absence rate of almost 30 per cent while a materials handling unit had one of less than 10 per cent. Nevertheless, the shop supervisor was unconcerned, while the unit supervisor was very worried. This was because the people in the shop were generally older and had four weeks' holiday entitlement per annum; and two of the people had been absent for several months, seriously ill. The unit, by contrast, employed younger people who had only two weeks' annual holiday entitlement. However, frequent, short and unpredictable absences on the part of almost all of the people there made the supervisor's job of planning work schedules a nightmare.

Most firms produce some kind of estimate of the time lost through absenteeism, but few of them look at the frequency of absenteeism — probably because the former measure is easier for accountants, who can easily estimate the cost of the time lost. However, if we are to be able to plan absence control, frequency rates are a much more useful figure.

Companies which work out the costs of absenteeism usually become much more concerned to control it. Sick pay represents only a portion of the total, since you also have to cost in the price of employing temporary replacements or paying existing staff overtime to cover for the absentee's duties. Absenteeism also generates extra work in other departments — for example, wages, personnel, medical and welfare. At seminars held by the Industrial Society in 1980 and 1981, participants who had costed the absenteeism in their own companies estimated that it cost them between £25 and £40 per person per day. Even in those days, and even using the lower figure, a company employing 1000 people and suffering a 10 per cent rate of lost time would be forfeiting over £600,000 per annum.

Incidentally, absence of a manager for a week or two is usually much less costly than that of a shopfloor worker whose duties must be covered.

Absence liability and resistance

Employees who are frequently off sick are usually late more frequently, are more likely to be absent for other reasons, have more accidents at work and visit the company surgery more often. Changes in personnel policy may change one of these factors, but measured in the long term the total amount of time lost through absence can remain remarkably constant both for individuals and for groups.

Many studies have shown that absence — sickness absence in particular — is distributed unequally among any group of staff. A few people, perhaps 5-10 per cent, account for about half the total absence, and a few people are never absent at all. The latter are by no means always the healthiest, and nor are the former necessarily suffering from chronic ill health.

This distribution was first described 60 years ago in studies of injuries at work, and it gave rise to the idea that some people were 'accident-prone'. This is not necessarily an inherent and unalterable characteristic of the individual, but unless there is some control it is true that a pattern of absenteeism, once established, tends to persist throughout the individual's working life. This has important implications for the design of effective control measures. You are misleading yourself if you think that the sickness absences among your team's members are always just 'the luck of the draw', especially if they become frequent. People's state of health is usually only one of the factors that decide whether or not they come to work and, indeed, whether or not they will consult their doctor.

Factors affecting absence

Before you, or the organisation's management in general, can start to plan a programme for absence control, it is essential to be aware of the more important factors that influence absence. Much of the research into this problem has been primarily concerned with sickness absence, but in practice the same factors affect absence for other causes. Many of the factors are interrelated and, while some are for all practical purposes fixed, most are, or could be, altered by management or supervisory action, and doing this can form part of your absence-control programme. However, you will never get anywhere if you cling on to the traditional prejudices — which are, in fact, all too easy to disprove. If your attitude is that absenteeism is 'all because they malinger' or that it is brought about by doctors being too willing to sign sick notes, you are unlikely to find any solution to the problem.

There are three main categories of causes. Although they are not entirely mutually exclusive, the categories can help us analyse the problem. The three types of factors are geographical (climate, region, ethnic considerations, social insurance, health services, epidemics, local unemployment, social attitudes, etc.), organisational (nature and size of the organisation, industrial relations, personnel policy, sick pay, supervisory quality, working conditions, environmental hazards, occupational health service, labour turnover, etc.) and personal (age, sex, occupation, personality, life crises, job satisfaction, medical condition, alcohol use, family responsibility, travel-time to work, social activities, etc.).

Geographical influences

The widely held view that rates of absenteeism in the UK are particularly high is a complete falsehood.

One study carried out in 1968 showed the UK rate to be the same as those in Germany and Poland and well below those in Holland and Sweden. Another, carried out in 1978 in the motor industry, showed that the UK rate was the lowest among the seven European countries surveyed. In 1981, a study carried out in another multinational showed the UK rate to be well below those in Italy, Sweden and Holland and a little below those in Germany and France.

Within the UK, there are well known regional differences — for example, sickness rates are about three times higher in Wales than they are in the South East and East Anglia — and these contrasts have been becoming more marked over the last twenty years or so. To some extent the differences can be explained by the predominant types of work done in the regions, but that is not the whole story. The Post Office surveyed absenteeism through the UK during 1975-77, and the results are revealing because, of course, Post Office employees do much the same sort of work wherever they live. Among men the highest absenteeism was found in Northern Ireland, followed by the North West, Wales, North East, Scotland, London, South West, Midlands, South East and, finally, the East. Almost exactly the same order prevailed among women, except that the North West had slightly higher absenteeism than Northern Ireland. Interestingly, the differences between the best and worst regions for absenteeism were much smaller for women than they were for men.

Another possible factor can be differences between ethnic groups, but these are difficult to analyse. Several studies done in the USA have always shown consistent ethnic differences in sickness absenteeism, and it is thought that these may be the product of differing cultural attitudes to health and disease. One point is worth bearing in mind: there is a widespread belief that immigrant workers take more time off than their indigenous colleagues, but in fact this is by no means generally true.

High local unemployment can reduce casual absenteeism if people feel that their job security is at threat, but also sickness rates tend to be higher in depressed areas. A lot of people thought the huge rise in unemployment over the last few years would markedly reduce absence levels, but in fact only in some companies have there been falls, and then only modest ones. It would seem that the social-security system and company sick-pay schemes may have altered attitudes from those typical of the pre-war period, when high unemployment certainly did reduce absenteeism.

The level of sickness benefit is another possible influence. The best documented studies have come from West Germany, where it has been shown that shortly after each increase in the state benefit the rates of sickness absence did indeed rise. For many organisations in this country, the sick-pay scheme is more important than the national benefit, and changes such as the introduction of Earnings Related Benefit Supplement and the rule that no benefit was to be paid during the first three days' sickness had no significant effect — in either direction.

The average length of a sickness absence has been falling steadily for a number of years, and there is good evidence that any dramatic rise in sickness absence following an increase in national or company benefit does not last: the level soon settles at a level only slightly higher than that prevailing before the change. Nevertheless, it is certainly unwise to make large increases in sick pay. It is far better to raise it more frequently but by small increments. A point worth noting is that, while sick-pay schemes do increase the frequency of absence, they tend to reduce the total number of days taken off by the employee. Also of interest in this connection is that absenteeism is less when the scheme is funded solely by the organisation than if it relies partly or wholly on employee contributions.

Seasonal factors also play a part. Obviously, sickness rates are highest in the winter — a point often forgotten when comparing absence figures.

Organisational influences

All forms of absenteeism are usually higher in larger firms than in smaller ones, and the same often applies to large and small units or departments. The idea of 'economy of scale' has led to a lot of takeovers and mergers in recent years, but in fact over-large companies can suffer losses in output through increased absenteeism. One point which many observers have failed to notice is that the overall size of the organisation may not be the important factor, rather the size of the working community to which individuals consider themselves to belong.

The attitude of management at all levels is, as you might expect, of crucial importance. One little-recognised aspect of management's attitude is the matter of the care and maintenance of plant and equipment, which can have a dramatic effect on absenteeism — not just because of injuries. Overall sickness rates rise if equipment is poorly looked-after, not to mention time lost through grievances and shopfloor arguments. Another largely ignored link between management and absenteeism is the extent to which people are moved about from pillar to post. A study among trainee nurses showed that nurses moved rapidly around between the wards were much more likely to be off sick or even to leave. So plans that place too great a reliance on employee flexibility, and which require frequent changes of workplace or of the make-up of working groups could well lead to higher absenteeism.

Of course, you, as a supervisor, cannot dictate overall management policy — although in a well run organisation you should be able to affect it. However, to your staff you are the face of management, and the quality of your supervision is one of the most important of all factors affecting absenteeism. It has been shown that high rates of absenteeism are generated in departments whose supervisors seldom if ever show appreciation of good work. It could be argued that supervisors are unlikely to be well disposed to persistent absentees, but usually if the absentee makes this complaint his or her colleagues independently corroborate it, even if they themselves are only rarely absent. Giving credit where credit is due is part of the art of being an effective, communicative supervisor.

You may or may not have control of the system adopted for classifying absence in your team. If you do, think about it carefully. For example, one company paid people who were off sick for a day, but docked two hours' wages if people were even just a couple of minutes late in the morning. Many people admitted that, if they were on their way to work and realised they were going to be late, they simply turned round and went home again! The policy was actively encouraging absenteeism.

Insistence on a doctor's note has little or no effect on sickness absence. Many managers used to believe that it stopped malingerers, and insisted on it for even just one day's absence. When the UK law was changed in 1981 so that people could certify themselves sick for up to a week the widely expected boom in short-term sickness absences simply did not occur. One possible reason for this might be that the change in the law forced organisations to take a much more active interest in their employees' absences.

Poor working conditions are generally believed to cause absences, but surveys show that, unless the environment is so bad as to be genuinely hazardous, it makes little difference. Most people's working conditions have steadily improved in recent decades, and yet absence rates have risen considerably. However, tedious, unvaried and undemanding work, even if performed in ideal surroundings, is a different matter: we shall return to it later. The introduction of open-plan offices can cause a temporary upturn in the rate of short-term sickness absences, possibly because people miss the intimacy of the smaller group. Badly designed open-plan offices can certainly lead to rapid staff turnover, at least in the short term.

The effect of a factory medical service is hard to establish. On the one hand, it saves a lot of time in the treatment of minor illnesses and injuries; on the other, just because it is easily accessible, people are more likely to stop work to have minor ailments treated. The tendency of some GPs to hand out sickness certificates for a week or even two for the most minor of ailments — seemingly regarding the week as the standard unit of time —

is infuriating for management and expensive for the National Insurance fund, and so a factory doctor with a more realistic attitude may be able to reduce absenteeism and at the same time help the patient, because a return to work often speeds recovery. Like it or not, though, in most cases of sickness absence the person who usually decides whether or not to work and when they are fit to work is not the doctor but the patient, although countries which require factory doctors to certify incapacity for work show a slower rate of increase in absenteeism than others, and this is probably no coincidence.

It is impossible to justify the introduction of a factory medical service in terms of strict economics. Any change in the absence rates might equally well be in response to the more enlightened style of management which introduced the service.

Personal influences

In industry women tend to have about twice as much sickness absence as men, although this does not apply in the professions, nor to the single career woman. Young employees are generally absent more often than their older colleagues, but the absences are usually brief. The length of each sickness absence tends to rise markedly after employees have reached the age of 50. In general, the group with the lowest absenteeism consists of men aged 40, single or married, working in staff positions. Status may be a factor here, since staff employees always show lower absenteeism statistics than manual workers.

In the UK, coalminers have three times as much sickness absence as the national average, labourers have double it, and farmers, teachers and managers have only half. Before you jump to conclusions, remember that a minor ailment such as a back-strain would not affect the manager's work but would certainly require a coalminer to lay off for a day or two in case the injury was exacerbated disastrously.

If people are working for more than 60 hours per week their sickness rates will be higher than usual. Due to the fact that all of us are different, however, no one has yet succeeded in establishing that there is a direct association between overtime and either accidents or illness. Where overtime is largely or entirely voluntary, the people who do it are rarely absent, although some may take the Monday off after a profitable weekend.

The effects of shift working have been studied in some depth.

Our body-clocks take a few days to adapt themselves to alterations in our working hours and in our sleeping patterns. After that, however, shift workers are — surprisingly — absent less often, for sickness or any other reason, than day workers in similar jobs. There is no reason to believe that shift workers are healthier: they simply tend to stay off work less. The explanation probably lies in the organisation of the work, with a greater sense of personal involvement and also greater responsibility towards the other members of the team.

It is worth noting in this context that self-employed people are not given to taking time off work. As one freelance designer said to me, 'I cannot afford the time to be sick'. With the close link between our brains and our bodies it may not be too fanciful to suppose that the bodies of highly motivated people get the message and are less prone to illness. A good supervisor will engender a climate in which everyone does feel that they are working for themselves as well as for the organisation, with the added benefit of working together as a team.

Perhaps the most important of all personal factors is employees' attitudes towards their job, their employer, their boss and their work group. Sixty years ago the psychiatrist Ronald Ross remarked that illness and absence from work were both behavioural modes adopted by an unhappy individual. Work in a frustrating job or for a difficult boss can adversely affect an individual's reaction to a minor illness and can also contribute to the development of a stress-related ailment — such as, at worst, cancer, alcoholism or heart disease. That said, you have to remember that what is tedious or frustrating for one person is deeply satisfying for another, so the problem is not necessarily one of making the job more exciting but one of fitting the right person to the right job.

The other personal factor that has a really major effect on absence is individuals' attitudes towards themselves. Often people with bad attendance records are found to have chips on their shoulders, and take the view that life has treated them badly. They tend to be preoccupied with minor disorders and have a low threshold for discomfort. While they are not malingerers, their hypochondria can lead to high absenteeism.

The time it takes an employee to get to work, if it is over about an hour, can affect sickness absence rates. A study of London office workers found that both the frequency and duration of sickness absences were increased for people whose daily journeys were complicated by several interchanges. One-day sickness was, for some reason, higher in those using a car for part or all of the journey.

Alcohol abuse (perhaps to the extent of alcoholism) is also an important and frequently unrecognised factor. Poor timekeeping, prolonged lunch hours and single-day absences because of 'headaches' and 'gastric problems' can progress to lengthy absences due to serious ill-health. Unfortunately, heavy drinkers are often shielded by colleagues, and a problem that could have been easily tackled early on may become an addiction. A declared company policy on alcohol, encouraging people to seek help without being victimised, can do a great deal. In the USA many companies allow their more senior employees fully paid leave to attend centres specialising in curing drink problems, the fees for which are paid by the company.

As we have noted once or twice, the actual physical health of employees is often quite unconnected with their amount of absenteeism. The routine examination given before someone is taken on is useless in predicting subsequent absence due to illness. Even people with chronic and/or disabling conditions may work for years without missing a day, while the healthiest employee can easily break a leg playing football or suffer from constant minor ailments.

Finally, family problems and responsibilities can have an effect. As a supervisor you will be able to cite many such examples, but many of us tend to forget that some employees with exactly the same problems never miss a day's work. For example, marital discord can positively drive a person to work — particularly if he or she derives job satisfaction from it.

The control of absenteeism

A few years ago a survey of 71 companies revealed that there were 41 different techniques of absence control in use, none of which, of course, could be guaranteed to be effective in every situation: with so many factors affecting absence rates, it would be naive to expect a single, universal panacea.

Few companies have any coordinated plan of absence control. Most try to control one or two forms of absence, but other forms — notably sickness absence — are largely neglected as uncontrollable. Attempts to reduce or control one or two forms of absenteeism are usually ineffective, in that the absenteeism just takes on different forms, while a rigid policy that sets out to catch the malingerer at all costs will frustrate or irritate conscientious employees and actually bring about an overall increase in absenteeism.

As we have seen, absenteeism is both a characteristic of groups of employees and something dependent on each individual's attitudes. Any plan to control it must therefore consider both group absenteeism and individual absenteeism. Any comprehensive plan for absence control should have two principal components:

- creating an improved climate of interest and concern throughout the organisation
- addressing itself towards the specific techniques used under different circumstances and for different types of absence

At the supervisory level there is little you can do about the first of these components, although you can operate within your own team to estimate the costs of absenteeism (remembering the points we made in this context on page 51) and to find out whether or not the problem is really serious. If it is, and if the costs are high, you should agitate for some authority from higher up to do something about it. For the next few pages we shall discuss techniques in the company-wide context, bearing in mind that many of them are applicable also on the smaller scale.

Many firms make no effort to analyse absence; others make remarkably complicated measures on a monthly, weekly or even daily basis. Of these two extremes, the former is sometimes preferable. Elaborate studies of hours lost are useless without measures of frequency rates, since a single person absent for a month from a small group can radically distort the group's figures for that month. Similarly, as we noted, seasonal effects mean that results for periods of less than a full year are difficult to interpret unless you have available the comparable figures for earlier years. In general, then, it is not worth while to produce figures for a group of people unless, when you multiply the number of people by the time-period considered, you end up with a result of about 50 person-years or more. Since there should be no more than about 15 people in a supervisor's team, this means that your own survey period should be three or four years, which is probably too long (if nothing else, you are likely to be further up the management ladder before you can finish your survey). However, you can make realistic comparisons between two years if you, for example, discount the fact that in one of them someone was recovering from a heart attack or whatever and so was off work for an extended period. Another thing management must watch when comparing different groups is that they may not be comparing like with like: as we have seen, factors such as sex, status, age and the type of task involved can mean that one group has inherently quite different absenteeism behaviour from another.

The manner in which statistics are compiled and presented is worth attention — particularly to you as a supervisor. If you tell your people that 'the company had an absence rate of 7¾ per cent for the last three months' this does not mean a lot, but if you say that 'every day for the last three months over 100 people were absent' people will sit up and take notice.

The organisation as a whole and you in particular should aim to control absenteeism by giving the maximum possible job satisfaction to all employees. This may seem idealistic, but in fact it is not: any improvement is better than none. Studies in applied psychology have shown that most employees wish to do a good job, and that very few are genuinely temperamentally unsuited to long-term employment. You can do a lot for local job satisfaction — give praise where it is due, be fun to work for, and so on — but as far as the organisation is concerned, overall job satisfaction is something that has to be imposed from the top downwards: the happier your boss is, the happier you will be, and so the happier your team will be. Management must go about this in two ways:

- fostering an atmosphere in which serious discussion about individuals' jobs and working relationships is encouraged
- carrying out a detailed analysis and making changes in areas where the need is greatest (knowledge of absence rates, assuming they are corrected for such factors as status and age, can be a great help here)

One problem is that managers and supervisors can in themselves be a major source of job dissatisfaction, and little progress can be made until these individuals are persuaded, first, that there is a problem and, second, that they must play their part in solving it. Some will have the old-fashioned view that increasing discipline is the only solution; presumably you are not one of these, as otherwise you would hardly be likely to be reading this book.

Certainly there is a clear need for improving the selection and training of all supervisory staff — a matter to which we shall return in Chapter Six. A related difficulty is that there is no truly reliable way of assessing a person's capacity, and all too often inadequacy in a manager or supervisor becomes apparent only when that person has been promoted above the level of his or her ability.

Many manual workers with bad absence records are frustrated at work and would cetainly improve if they were given more responsibility. Unfortunately, a person with a bad absence record is likely to have difficulty gaining promotion. Some seek satisfaction outside their jobs and, if they are successful, their work attendance may improve. A very few have personality problems, and sadly there is not much you can do for them except to give occasional words of encouragement or praise: almost everyone responds well to this whereas few of us improve our performance when threatened.

For most people the requirements for job satisfaction, assuming they are being paid a living wage, are as follows:

- the work should offer some element of challenge
- they should know exactly what their job is and how they are performing
- in some area of their job they should be allowed to make decisions
- the work should be organised in such a way that they can call on the support and assistance of their colleagues when they need it
- they should have some idea of how their job fits into the overall department or company picture
- there should be the prospect of a desirable future, in terms of either promotion, security, stable income or increased skills — or all of these
- they should have some recognised status

All of these elements should be kept in mind by management when assessing policies and techniques of making alterations in departments, work groups and individual jobs. As an example of what can be achieved in this area, two groups of miners employed in similar areas of the same pit were compared over several years. The first worked according to the conventional system of job-oriented work patterns, while the members of the second were allowed to reorganise the tasks among themselves, without imposition from above. Needless to say, the output of the second group was higher and the incidence of absence and accidents much lower.

If management is to take tactical action to control absenteeism, identifying the problem areas is vital. Absence is ultimately a function of the individual employee, but units and departments tend to show a relatively stable frequency of absence. Too many absence-control programmes in industry are both inefficient and out of date. Clearly, if managers are to concentrate their resources where action is most needed, they require not just statistics but meaningful statistics. Since the pattern of absence has changed during the last couple of decades, with short-duration, high-frequency spells causing most of the problem, it no longer makes sense to concentrate on the few employees who are off work for long periods. Managers should ensure that the medical, welfare and front-line supervisors work closely together and not, as is so often the case, in isolation from each other.

Absence control is a management responsibility for which the help of specialists is essential — and you are one of those specialists.

Tactics for absence control

Changing the climate of a plant or office with regard to absence is largely a question of manipulating group attitudes. Tactics for absence control are concerned more with individuals.

Obviously, those individuals need to be identified, but this is easy enough if one simply looks back through the records. Often you will find that a person has sustained a high absence rate for many years, and this can be tricky: the person may quite justifiably ask why there is a sudden change in the organisation's attitude to his or her absenteeism now, when in the past it was acceptable. In this context there are two things worth considering: the correct use of the period of trial employment, and the attitudes of the employee's colleagues.

In most industrial organisations the idea of an initial trial period is included in the contract of employment (although, to be fair, in some industries, such clauses are rare because no one will sign contracts containing them). After six months in the job, the employee has greater security under the Employment Protection Act. If a new employee takes frequent spells of absence, certified or not, and the appointment is then confirmed, it could reasonably be argued that his or her record would have to deteriorate substantially before dismissal for absenteeism could be justified. There is also good evidence that the only accurate way of predicting future absenteeism is to look at the past record. Six months or a year is quite long enough to recognise a 'repeater', and the individual should be warned within the trial period that continued absenteeism is likely to lead to early dismissal. The trial period, after all, should be seen as a trial of health and attendance as well as of ability. Of course, if a person genuinely suffers from poor health, you might think of transferring that person to a different section where the ailments would have less effect in terms of absences; as we noted earlier, ailments which necessarily keep a person off work in one area may be merely minor irritations in another.

The attitudes of a persistent absentee's colleagues are something you overlook at your peril, and you, as a supervisor, are in the best position of anyone in management to know what these are. People on the shop floor are the first to recognise that one of their number is abusing sick-leave privileges, and most of them strongly disapprove; however, loyalty usually inhibits them from expressing their views to managers. If managers appear to condone the behaviour (and all too often, let us face it, they have not even noticed it) the colleagues become resentful and develop the attitude of: 'Well, if X can get away with it, why shouldn't we do it too?' The situation is then likely to get out of hand.

Once defaulting individuals have been identified, there are then, in essence, only three ways of tackling the problem, used separately or in combination. They are rewards, punishments, and exhortations or individual counselling. Since, as we have seen, there are a vast number of possible reasons for absenteeism, their possible permutations with these three methods are almost infinite. Some techniques are described as gimmicks, but there is nothing wrong with a gimmick that works! Any long-term programme should allow for the fact that the techniques used will change over time: no single technique of absence control will remain effective for ever.

Using rewards to reduce absenteeism is often criticised on the basis that, if employees are already being paid to be at work, why should they be paid again? However logical this might seem, the fact remains that, for any working group, there is an unwritten norm of absence: if you want to reduce this norm, one method is to provide an incentive. The good-attendance bonus, in various forms, has undoubtedly proved effective in a wide variety of companies. When introducing such a scheme, however, there are two main problems to be overcome:

- the definition of a justifiable reason to be absent without affecting one's bonus
- the determination of the length of the absence-free period required if one is to qualify for the bonus

Successful bonus schemes usually work best in small or medium-sized firms, of up to a few hundred employees; in larger firms, apart from anything else, the administrative costs become prohibitive. The most satisfactory schemes appear to be those linked to the individual, and in which a certain small amount of absence still allows the employee to claim at least part of their bonus. Even when a scheme does work, however, the beneficial effect tends to wear off after a year or two. Some firms find that their employees eventually demand that the bonus be incorporated into their basic wage. On balance, then, bonus schemes are not to be recommended.

Punishments are a traditional sanction in industry, and on this count alone one can question their usefulness, bearing in mind that despite them absenteeism has continued to rise. The ultimate sanction is dismissal, and companies vary widely in their willingness to use it. The deterrent effect of the threat of dismissal depends largely on the state of the local labour market as it affects the individual. Since, in terms of frequency, the worst absenteeism offenders tend to be young, single, unskilled labouring men, who are probably most likely to find it easiest to change jobs, the threat of dismissal may not be a particularly effective one. Also, sometimes employees with a poor attendance record work very well when they are actually there, so that any replacement, even if with a perfect attendance record, might in fact be less efficient. For example, one county-council executive arrives late every morning, spends much of his time in the office reading the newspaper, takes a protracted lunch-hour and leaves the office spot-on five o'clock each evening, yet he still gets through 50 per cent more work than most of his colleagues: would it make any sense to threaten him with dismissal?

Other, less drastic, punishments include threats or admonishments and the withholding of privileges such as entry to pension schemes or sick-pay entitlements.

Ten or more years ago few companies had defined policies about absenteeism which saw as their end-point the possibility of dismissal. Many managers felt that certified absences simply had to be tolerated, although a few organisations, including the Post Ofice, did have laid-down agreements (accepted, incidentally, by the unions) in which dismissal for 'irregular attendance' was agreed as a final sanction. It may not be a coincidence that absenteeism in the Post Office has failed to rise at the same speed as in other organisations over the last couple of decades.

Since the introduction of the Employment Protection Act, industrial tribunals and the Employment Appeal Tribunal, case law has created a set of guidelines which permit managers to dismiss employees for persistent absenteeism or for recurrent certified sickness absence. For such dismissal to be accepted as fair, the employer must have behaved 'reasonably', which means that the persistent absentee must have been clearly warned and given an opportunity to improve. When genuine ill-health appears to be the underlying reason, you or any other manager should obtain medical advice, consider more suitable alternative work for the employee, and, most important of all, allow the employee to have his or her say. Agreement with trade unions along these lines is now quite commonplace: other employees, as we have noted, are the first who resent a colleague abusing sick-leave regulations. Dismissal on the grounds of an unacceptable attendance record may still be a rare event, but the existence of a reasonable yet unequivocal company policy which allows for this as a last resort can make a tremendous difference to management's task — and, for that matter, your task — in controlling abuse.

Obviously punishments must be meted out on the same terms to all. Alas, most of the sanctions in use have least effect on those who most require to be penalised. Often, in companies where penalties for lateness are imposed, offenders can easily make up the fine by working a little overtime: the clock cards of some of the worst offenders bear witness to the futility of the penalty.

Sadly, the idea that you can use the sick-pay scheme or the pension scheme to control absenteeism has yet to die the death. The notion that employees should suffer financially when genuinely sick is still held by many. As we have seen, the introduction of generous sick-pay schemes is usually associated with a short-term increase in sickness absences, but the evidence shows that the situation levels out fairly soon. To give a single example of why the 'high sick pay equals high absenteeism' argument falls down, we can note that staff employees generally receive more generous sick pay than manual labourers, and yet their absence levels are almost always lower.

The view dies hard that people will come to work only when they risk starvation or a visit from the bailiffs. Many companies operate a paradoxical system whereby stern discipline and the withholding of wages are applied when people are absent for social or family reasons, whereas people who are absent for medical reasons receive full pay. This is unfair, and the effect of such policies is obvious: the employee finds a medical reason for his or her absence. The enforcement of such a system is simply luring employees into quite understandable petty dishonesty.

Nowadays it is common for managers and supervisors to explain high absenteeism in terms of 'malingering'. The word should in fact be appied only to those who deliberately feign illness in order to skive off work. In fact, in terms of overall absenteeism, malingering is fairly unimportant, as most factory doctors would agree. Most people who have bad sickness records fail to report for work because they genuinely do feel ill, and any delays in their return to work are usually because they do not yet feel fully recovered. Be careful before you start to regard one of your team as a malingerer.

A different sanction, but one that can be effective if used sensibly, relates to overtime. If someone has a high absenteeism record during normal time, and yet clocks up a lot of overtime, it is reasonable to point out that the overtime is having an adverse effect upon their health and that therefore they ought to stick to normal working hours. Shop stewards will usually agree that this is a reasonable move, if briefed in advance.

There are other techniques, involving neither rewards nor punishments, that can be efficacious in the control of absenteeism. These may be directed either at groups or at the individual, but undoubtedly the most effective are those directed at the individual. For example, the publicising of absence rates, in terms that are meaningful for your team, can have a considerable impact. You might post a notice like the one shown on the following page:

ABSENCE
The factory average last year was four absences per person. One third of the employees had no absences at all. Workers in our department averaged six absences each, and 25 people were absent on more than 20 occasions.
ABSENCE LOWERS PRODUCTIVITY, INCREASES COSTS, AND THUS AFFECTS YOUR WAGE PACKET

Interviews with poor attenders should ideally be done by yourself. If you want to achieve a constructive result you should ensure that the discussion is not recriminatory. As poor attenders often have high sickness-absence rates there is something to be said for having the interview carried out by the medical officer or nursing sister. In many cases this can be of inestimable value, since the root causes of the poor attendance record can be discovered and, with luck, remedied.

Another useful tactic of control is the sick visit. Several studies have shown that a visit paid to the employee at home on the first or second day of the illness has a marked effect. However, you have to take care as to how you carry out the visit, since you do not want to give the impression that you are on a spying mission: that simply creates resentment. Although one's first thoughts about visiting sick employees might be that they are a way of encouraging the longer-term ill to return to work a week or two early, in fact you can save your organisation more absence time if you include people with short-term illnesses in your visits. For example, in a factory with an annual sickness rate of 11 days per employee it was calculated that, if absence spells of a month were shortened by a week, the total time lost would fall by 2 per cent; in contrast, were every absence spell shortened by only a single day, the saving would be 15 per cent. These figures should not be taken too literally, as any statistician will tell you, but their general import is clear.

Visiting your team members who are ill has a further advantage. The very fact that you have turned up to express your concern about their illness is likely to motivate them. You are the front line of management, and you are showing that management cares.

It is curious that most companies expect sick employees to return to work on a Monday. In fact, especially when people have been off for a few weeks, it makes much more sense for them to return on a Wednesday or a Thursday, so that they can have a couple of days at work before the weekend, rather than having to work a full week while perhaps not feeling totally recovered. Another way of easing the process of returning to work is to allow people to work reduced hours for the first few days, perhaps in conjunction with a modification of the work they are expected to do. Remember, there is always a transitionary period between being totally unfit and being totally fit; if you expect your people to wait until they are totally fit before they come back to work you are not only wasting your company's money, you are hindering the process of the individual's return to fitness: a few hours' work a day, as you must know from your own experience, is an excellent way of making you feel better after a long illness.

After they have been off sick for a considerable time, some people can actually be afraid of returning to work. This is most likely when people have been absent for 6-10 weeks, and is commonest when the employee either was at risk of death (as with a heart attack) or suffered an occupational injury. The psychological reasons for this fear of returning to work are complex, but we can sum them up as a form of depression brought about by a combination of the illness itself, the social isolation that prolonged absence from work involves, and the accompanying delusion that the firm does not really want the person back. Frequent visits to such employees, during which you can discuss ways of easing them back into the saddle, can be of considerable help. In such cases, however, past attendance records can be misleading: a person with a poor record may be eager to return to work at the first possible opportunity, whereas someone with a good record may require much longer to recover, and may at first be able to work only for shortened hours.

Many other tactics of controlling sickness absence have been used, some of which have a scientific basis whereas others involve real or fancied fringe benefits. For example, influenza-immunisation programmes reduce absenteeism through genuine cases of 'flu, but have no effect on absenteeism brought about by other conditions of the upper respiratory tract. Moreover, except among senior staff, only about 40 per cent of employees in large organisations accept such programmes. Since vaccines against 'flu are of limited effectiveness — regular epidemics occur usually because a new virus, undaunted by the vaccine, has come into being — the cost of the immunisation programme may be greater than the amount of money saved. Likewise, no one has yet come up with a cure for the common cold.

Such statements ignore something important: the 'placebo

effect' can reduce absenteeism. It is well known to doctors that simply giving someone a pill — any pill — can help them get better, and so the mere fact that management is seen to care for the employees can reduce time taken off for sickness. In the period 1971-76 the Post Office offered 60,000 employees vaccine against 'flu each winter, and surveyed the results, comparing the absence records of the groups offered the vaccine with those who had not been. Even though the acceptance rate in the groups offered the vaccine was only about 30 per cent, those groups showed a significantly lower rate of absenteeism than the others. Intriguingly, this reduction was observable not just during 'flu epidemics but also both before and afterwards. Cost-benefit analyses indicated that the programme was making significant savings, and so free vaccination was offered annually to all employees. Over the succeeding five years the acceptance rate fell steadily (probably, in part, because there were no 'flu epidemics during those years), and when it had dropped to around 10 per cent the justification for continuation became questionable. However, over the years, the programme had saved the Post Office a very great deal of money.

Smaller organisations are likely to find that up to 40 per cent of staff will be interested in such a programme, and so annual offers of free immunisation are probably worthwhile.

Conclusions

Effective control of absenteeism requires three things:

- information
- correct managerial attitudes
- appropriate policies and procedures

Managers and supervisors must have records which contain details of individuals' absences, and must also have the awareness and ability to analyse groups whose members are likely to run the greatest risk of high absenteeism. They should measure not only the duration of absences but also, much more important, their frequency, and have a realistic idea of how much absenteeism costs. Finally, they should be able to identify problem areas and individuals, so that action can be concentrated where it is most needed. This last point is a particular concern of yours, as a supervisor.

The matter of attitudes refers to whether absenteeism. taken seriously by the top management — and, if so, do workforce know that this is the case? Do high-frequency absent realise that management is only too well aware of their existence? In both of these areas your role as a supervisor is vital.

Finally, appropriate policies and procedures include salary and employment policies that encourage attendance, internal standards of acceptable absence levels, and stated criteria for action when these are exceeded. There must be agreed procedures for dealing with poor attenders. Where necessary, medical advice should be sought to establish appropriate preventive measures in the field of occupational health.

The control of absenteeism is the responsibility of management — at all levels, including that of the supervisor. The personnel department and any occupational health service can be only advisory and supportive: it really is up to you and the people further up the management level. As we have seen in this chapter, there are many contributions you can make to the control of absenteeism, but the greatest you can make is (if possible) to improve people's enjoyment of and involvement with their work. Of course, the last thing you want to do is to encourage people with an infectious disease to stagger in dozily to try to carry out their functions — that's a recipe for increasing both absenteeism among the other staff and absenteeism of the individual through industrial injury. However, if someone is really involved in what they are doing and genuinely motivated, they will return to work much earlier than otherwise — indeed, may never go sick — and may as a result recover their health more swiftly.

Which is good for them, good for you, and good for the organisation — the three aims of the effective supervisor.

5 INDUCTION

Induction is the process whereby new recruits are integrated into an organisation so that as soon as possible they become active, cooperative and productive members of it. It is one of the great neglected areas of management policy. Each year in Britain hundreds of thousands — if not millions — of pounds are wasted on recruiting and training people who leave their jobs long before they have contributed anything like what they potentially could to their organisation. Of course, not all of this wastage can be blamed on poor induction, but a great deal of it can, particularly in the case of young employees.

New members of your team naturally want to know who their colleagues are, who is their boss (and their boss's boss), how they fit into the organisation, and how their own and their department's work relates to that of other people and other departments. They want to know what the organisation's aims are and, in general terms, how it is organised. They need to have a variety of basic data about such things as the terms and conditions of their employment, trade-union membership, and the layout of their working environment.

All of these things should be part of an organisation's induction scheme, but quite frequently there is not even any checkable drill or routine for inducting an employee. If you expect new recruits simply to pick things up as they go along, or if you hope that the traditional 'tour with handshakes' will be enough, you are simply asking for the newcomer to adopt an attitude of indifference to the organisation's success: the person's stay with you is likely to be a short one.

Staff turnover costs money. Related problems such as lack of effort, indifference and absenteeism cost even more. All of them represent unacceptable wastage of an organisation's human resources — the most valuable asset it has. Good induction schemes do not provide the whole of the answer, but without them there is certainly no answer at all.

72

In some form or another, the process of induction always takes place, but frequently it is haphazard and inefficient. As with any form of communication, it will be far more effective if it is properly managed and planned. The advantages of a planned induction scheme can hardly be questioned. An experiment carried out some years ago by the Texas Instruments plant in Bedford compared ten new recruits receiving a full induction with a control group of ten recruits who received the 'normal treatment'. After one month's working, the differences were staggering:

	Experimental group	Control group
units produced per hour	93	27
absence rate	0.5%	2.5%
number of times late	2	8
training hours undergone	225	381

Many other benefits — apart from the obviously huge savings in costs — derived from this scheme when the company adopted it as a general policy: higher quality, better communication and lower staff turnover were only three.

In order to devise an induction action-plan, management has to consider three principal questions:

● what should we tell them?
● who should tell them?
● when should they be told?

The part you play as a supervisor is vital in all three areas. Let us look at them in turn.

What to tell them

There are three main categories of information new recruits need to know:
● job information
● personal information
● team information

By 'job information' we mean the things the recruits need to know if they are to do their jobs effectively. This may involve a training programme, but often it is largely a question of simple orientation. As well as informing recruits of what they have to do, it is obviously vital to tell them why it is important and how their work fits in with that of the department and that of the organisation as a whole.

The term 'personal information' refers to those things that affect a recruit's private life and individual needs: obvious examples are how to collect wages, where the canteen is and where the loos are. It is not only embarrassing for the new recruit to have to ask you about such fundamentals, it adds to the stresses and anxieties which everybody feels when they join a new organisation.

Finally, you need to give new recruits 'team information' — that is, a knowledge of all those things that will speed up the person's integration into the working group. It is important that you should cover not just the formal but the informal aspects of working life within the team: the fact that you all go for a pint after work on a Friday is just as important to the new recruit as the details of who the employee representative is, what the team's overall role is, and even who you — the supervisor — are.

Who should tell them

The golden rule in induction is that, if in doubt, the person who should pass on information to a new recruit is the person's immediate boss — that is, you, the person's supervisor. You are the person who has the greatest vested interest in the recruit's speedy induction, and you are the person responsible for ensuring that the recruit is given the right balance of information about the job, personal factors and the team, and will maintain the correct balance in his or her work. Also, the situation gives you an ideal opportunity to establish a good working relationship with the new recruit and to make it perfectly clear that you really are the 'source of authority' and the leader of the department — at the same time as, of course, basically making friends.

The induction of a new recruit is one of the very few examples of a task that should never be delegated. However, there are two other people in the department who may play a role: the employee representative and a specially appointed sponsor.

Whether or not the recruit is a member of a trade union, the staff representative should be asked to tell the person about joint consultative and grievance procedures. This explanation need not be in any great depth, but the recruit should be made aware of the fact that they exist and understand the mechanics of taking the first step towards invoking them. If the recruit is a union member, the staff representative should explain the union rule book.

The induction process can be considerably assisted if you appoint a sponsor, or counsellor, for the new recruit. The sponsor should be another member of the team, and should be of the same sex and roughly the same age as the recruit. Obviously, you want as sponsor someone who will be conscientious about it. It can be of great assistance for a new recruit to have a ready-made 'friend' to turn to, particularly in the areas of personal information and group integration: every working group develops its own unwritten rules of behaviour, and for a recruit unwittingly to contravene these can give rise to both embarrassment and humiliation.

Increasingly, organisations find themselves recruiting outside their own geographical area, and in such cases the sponsor can perform an invaluable role in introducing the newcomer to the community. Obviously, for this, you should select a sponsor whose interests at least overlap with those of the recruit.

A useful side-effect of the appointment of sponsors is that is not just good for the new recruit: the sponsor, too, can benefit considerably, and become a likely candidate for promotion.

Other people can play a smaller part in induction. The role of the personnel department should be minimal and confined to 'specialist' areas, such as explaining details of the contract of employment, the pension and sickness schemes, and so on. The personnel department is also the obvious candidate if the recruit is to undergo any formal training session concerning the company's history and background.

Finally, it is a good idea if the recruit has a short interview with your immediate boss. This will help the person recognise more senior management and appreciate the role of the department. The practice also gives your boss the opportunity of meeting every new recruit and monitoring the effectiveness of the way you are carrying out the induction programme.

75

When they should be told

Induction is a continuing process. Any attempt to tell the recruit everything at once, especially in a 'classroom' atmosphere, is destined for disaster. Induction seems to be best spread over three main time periods:

- before the recruit joins up
- the first day of employment
- the first fortnight of employment
- the first six weeks of employment

The personnel department will play its major induction role in the period before the recruit arrives: they will have to explain, either in writing or both verbally and in writing, details of the contract of employment, working hours, pay, pension and sickness schemes, joining arrangements, date, time, place, travel arrangements, parking facilities, and so on. You too should be involved at this stage, since you — not the personnel department — are going to be the person with whom the recruit will work: ideally you will have been involved in or totally responsible for appointing them in the first place. At some time before the person joins your team you should show them the geography of the department and introduce them to the person who is to be their sponsor. You should also make a definite arrangement for you and the recruit to have an introductory meeting on the person's first morning at the job; if the nature of the department creates difficulties, there is no need why you cannot fix up to have this meeting somewhere else — even in the reception area.

It is your duty to make sure that everything is prepared for the recruit's arrival. All equipment, clothing, safety wear, etc., must be ready, and anyone else whom you want the recruit to meet on his or her first day should be informed of the fact, told the time of day when they must expect the recruit, and told how long you expect the meeting to go on.

If your preparations have been thorough, day one of the new recruit's employment should go smoothly. Avoid trying to tell them too much on the first day: it is enough simply to outline the things about which will you will brief them more thoroughly in the days and weeks to come.

You should be ready and available to meet the new recruit at the start of the day, and should tackle with them all the essentials of working in your organisation and team: clocking on (if applicable), coats, locker room, cloakroom, fire and safety precautions, smoking restrictions, safety measures, the nature of the job, introductions to the other team members ... all the things you might expect. Never deputise this task: the recruit will quite justifiably be offended, and that is hardly the best way to initiate a good working relationship. However, at tea and meal breaks, it is a good idea if you let the recruit's appointed sponsor take over: not only does this give the recruit the opportunity of asking questions he or she may not like to ask you directly (such as whether or not you are really this friendly all the time!) but it also allows you the chance of swiftly coping with anything urgent that may have come up in your own work.

If recruits are already skilled in the type of work they are doing, you should allow them some time on their own during the first day so that they can familiarise themselves with the new environment, the equipment they will be expected to use, and so on. It may well be, however, that the recruit needs training, in which case there are other things to do — see below.

All of these activities are ones that the recruit might expect to do in a typical day on the job, but you should also arrange a few extras on the first day. For example:

- a brief talk (five minutes at most) with the staff representative — you can arrange for a more extended meeting to take place later
- a quick visit to the medical room and/or factory doctor
- a trip to where the recruit will be paid, and an introduction to the people responsible for pay-cheques; even if the recruit is to be paid by direct draft, it is important that he or she know the people whose job it is to arrange this, in case there are any problems later

After the first day but during the first fortnight the process of induction should continue, although by now of course the recruit will be working almost full time on the job in question. Again, the induction process should be as natural as possible. This means that you have to cover all the points at the right time — i.e., when they are most relevant. If recruits are already skilled in the work, they will want to spend much of their time practising their skills — indeed, this is the best way for them to discover the work requirements and find acceptance within the team. So that disruption to the natural induction process can be kept to a minimum, any formal induction sessions should be fixed by appointment well in advance; this allows you time to prepare material and the recruit time to prepare questions. Otherwise both of you are likely to think of important matters after the session is over.

The things about which the recruit will want to know at this stage are likely to include such items as work targets and overtime arrangements: something that it is all too easy for you to forget about is the matter of disciplinary procedures (*see* Chapter Three). Too often people do not know what the disciplinary procedure is until it is invoked. Also, explain the procedures for joint consultation and complaints. The first fortnight is the appropriate time for the recruit's extended interview with the staff representative, but these vital points should be covered by you, not just by the representative.

Other appointments which you can make for the recruit during the first fortnight include one with the personnel department, where the workings of sick-pay schemes, pensions, savings schemes and social and sports-club facilities can be explained. Towards the end of the first fortnight is about the right time to fix up a meeting between the recruit and your own boss. The subject of this will be primarily the organisation of the department, with stress on the way that the various elements work together and communicate so that the desired result is achieved.

So much for the first fortnight. By the end of the sixth week the recruit should be getting into a steady work routine: their performance levels should be climbing steadily and they should be settling in as a member of the team. That this is indeed the case is something you should verify through observation and analysis and directly through your daily dealings with the recruit; regular conversations with the recruit's sponsor can also help you check on the situation.

However, there may still be some things you need to get across. For example:

- education and training facilities
- promotion and transfer possibilities
- special arrangements for booking holidays, both annual and statutory (unless you have covered these earlier)

At some stage during the first six weeks there should also be a formal 'welcome' meeting, arranged by the personnel or training department, conducted by a member of senior management, and attended by all recent arrivals in the organisation regardless of their age or status. Plainly there should be a reasonable number of people at such meetings, so they should not be held too frequently unless the organisation has a very high rate of staff turnover or is just very large. Often the senior manager conducting the meeting attempts to command loyalty among the new recruits simply by discussing the history and structure of the company, but this is a mistake: loyalty is something that has to be earned. The best approach may be to present a sort of straightforward ad for the company: this is what we make, this is what our products are used for, and this is how both you and the consumer benefit. By all means the manager should feel free to discuss the relevance of each department represented there (and others, if necessary), but the recruits will be much more impressed if they are told that the company is doing something worthwhile now than they will be by an account of who founded it, when it was founded, how it coped with the post-war years ... zzzzzzzzzz.

Some special cases

The guidelines given above cover all cases. There are, however, a few types of recruit who require special treatment — in addition to, not instead of, the things we have described. The three categories we shall discuss here are

- trainees
- graduates
- young people — i.e., school-leavers

Special measures must be taken for trainees joining your team if the training is to be partly or wholly off the job. However great the proportion of the recruit's time spent away from the job in training, you must still ensure that you have enough time to carry on the recruit's induction programme. The point here is that you are the person for whom the trainees will work, and so you have a vital interest in the effectiveness of their training and should be given time to ensure that the trainees develop a sense of belonging to your team even before they properly become a part of it.

Regular visits to your department by the trainees should help to minimise any adjustment problems they might have later, since they will be able to see their future colleagues doing the things about which they are currently learning. The frequency of such visits will obviously depend on the exact nature and duration of the training, but they should be organised in such a way that, by the time the trainees arrive in your department, you have gone through with them at least the stages of induction we described above as suitable for the pre-employment phase and the first day.

When planning the induction of graduates it is important to differentiate between those who have been recruited purely for their technical expertise and those who have been recruited as potential managers. In either case, although for different reasons, emphasis needs to be placed on matters of interdepartmental cooperation.

Engineers, chemists and other 'technical' graduates often see their own objectives in terms of scientific perfection. In a way, there is nothing wrong with this — it is one of the reasons they were recruited in the first place — but they should not be allowed to believe that it is the whole story. They need to have a clear idea of the constraints under which they will be working. Since these are broadly commercial, it is necessary that they have a general understanding of finance, marketing and production, so that they can appreciate the commercial factors that affect their work.

Graduates recruited for their management potential need to get an understanding of the business as a whole, and this means they have to be involved in a programme designed to highlight the roles and interdependences of the different departments. It is important, nevertheless, that they have a real job to do in a specific department. They will probably report not to you, as their immediate supervisor, but to a senior manager appropriately placed to organise the necessary interdepartmental activity. Their sponsor should be selected on the same basis as before, although perhaps there should be a greater emphasis placed on those aspects concerned with community of interest. While it is necessary that these graduates undergo induction in various departments, the 'Cook's Tour' approach should be avoided, since it can lead to the recruit being underused at any one time, and therefore becoming bored. If the right balance is to be achieved, management should pay particular attention to the feedback from the sponsor.

The induction of school-leavers requires special care. We all know the traumatic effects of starting in a new job; as we have noted, one of your duties is to reduce the anxiety of a new recruit as swiftly as possible. But the trauma of starting a new job is as nothing compared with when it is your first job, when you are fresh out of school.

However, school-leavers have one big advantage: their capacity for absorbing knowledge. Whatever the intelligence of the school-leaver, they are still likely to be able to absorb new information more easily and more quickly than someone older. This means that you may be able to shorten the time spent on induction. Note, too, that school-leavers are generally fascinated by the work content of the job.

Especially with young people, but in fact with all recruits, there is an increasing need to place considerable emphasis not just on what should be done but on why it should be done, or why it should be done in a certain way. Remember the example we cited in Chapter Three of the young person responsible for an accident which cost a colleague an eye simply because no one had ever told him why something should not be done? If you explain the why of the matter you are more likely to obtain cooperation and compliance with the established procedures, because the young recruit will understand the reasoning behind the procedures.

An effective induction programme provides the first chance for young employees to receive attitude training, the object being to ensure that any initial interest and enthusiasm they might have is developed and encouraged. Your influence in this respect is important, because any positive or negative attitudes to the work will be transmitted to the young recruit. If you sincerely believe in the importance of the work, and communicate that belief to the youngster, you do more to enthuse the recruit than if you spend weeks mechanically churning through information on techniques and practices. Moreover, you must make a point of genuinely identifying with the needs and attitudes of the young employee. Cast your mind back to when you started your first job: how would you have liked your new boss to treat you?

In order to get the active cooperation of youthful employees you might consider a number of major extensions to the basic induction programme. For example, a continuing programme of attitude and character development can be built around courses that present a physical and mental challenge and that broaden the experience of young people and foster in them a positive attitude to their work — and to life as a whole. Alternatively, or as well, you could encourage young employees to form a 'youth forum' — basically, a club open to all the young people in the organisation. It can operate to provide education on the operation of the company (including, for example, talks and discussion with senior executives about 'what I do and why'); it can involve its members in community service and organise social activities — that is, activities organised by the young employees for themselves, not things organised by management which you think the kids might enjoy (they won't).

Many young people have no very clear idea of how their job will develop or how it relates to any pre-employment experience they might have had (many have none). You should always keep in mind the possibility of training young employees in particular skills: these can be skills of which the youngsters have had some knowledge before joining the organisation or skills which, in a general way, they might be expected to develop. Young people — just as with all other recruits — like to think that their boss and their organisation have an interest in their careers: if you demonstrate a readiness to develop individual aptitudes you will be showing that you, and your organisation, are indeed interested in the futures of these young people.

Induction in the office

In terms of induction, there are in general few differences between an office job and any other. However, certain extras should be borne in mind. These arise from the facts that between one office and the next there are differences in jargon, procedures and systems, and that offices are administrative units where it is only too easy for recruits to get the idea that what they are doing is unimportant or just being done for its own sake.

The most obvious product of an office is paper. Most office jobs are concerned with receiving, opening, passing on, typing, copying, duplicating and filing paper. It is necessary to convince the new recruit that all those pieces of paper actually matter, that without them the organisation would be unable to realise its aims and objectives.

The induction of new office employees cannot be simply the traditional practice of taking them all round the office, introducing them to everyone, showing them their desk and leaving it at that. The best way to go about it is to use the induction methods we have already discussed, slightly lengthening the amount of time allocated for the introductory conversations between the recruit and his or her new colleagues. As well as learning what it is that the whole concern is in business to do, starting with the recruit's own department, the recruit should be told by the head of (or some other senior person within) each department what it does, why, and in general terms how. Such meetings should be spread over the first week or two. Additionally, you need to allow ample time for new recruits to meet their colleagues and discuss with them their jobs: what they do, where they get their work from, where they send it to, and so on.

It is often useful to give new recruits a simple glossary of terms, perhaps coupled or combined with a directory of procedures. Procedural handbooks, as we noted in Chapter Three, have a habit of getting overlong, overcomplicated and out-of-date, but nevertheless they provide a simple and painless way of communicating the 'style' of a company, and prevent new recruits from thinking they have joined a sort of secret society which has every intention of staying secret. The glossary should explain any job titles and system or machine names whose meanings are not self-evident; ignorance of such things always embarrasses new employees, especially if this is their first job. Granted, school-leavers have a lot to learn, but a state of constant embarrassment is not a recognised teaching aid!

Induction for all

One of the interesting by-products of introducing a full induction programme is that, because so many existing employees are involved, you discover that there are gaps in their knowledge, too. For example, in one wool-processing company it was discovered that an employee who had been there for ten years had no idea what actually happened in another department, despite the fact that her boss visited it frequently. Another operator asked: 'Why do new employees know more about this company after a week than I do after two years?' Obviously no induction programme had been conducted for those employees who had provided good and faithful service over the years, but who nevertheless remained sublimely ignorant of their own important roles in the company's achievement of its objectives.

Usually induction starts off with specialists, who give basic training to the new recruits. This training is supported by a follow-up programme conducted by supervisors, who are armed with a check-list. As a general rule, only about 20 per cent of the training will 'stick', so the onus on supervisors to ensure that the recruits become fully equipped with the necessary information is very heavy. It is therefore vital that supervisors know about the whole of the induction programme, as opposed to just ticking things off on their check-list.

Experienced supervisors, as well as newly appointed ones, faced with conducting their own induction programme often ask questions like these:

- how do I prepare an induction programme?
- what are the priorities?
- when do I conduct my sessions?
- I'm no training expert, so how do I go about it?

Induction programmes are a good thing for *all* employees, not just new recruits, but they need careful planning. If new recruits are to be properly inducted, management must ensure that existing employees are fully conversant with the organisation as a whole. Likewise, management must make sure that supervisors are told about or have experience of an induction programme before expecting them to conduct a similar programme for the new recruits. Preferably supervisors should have an in-company induction course prior to the launching of the induction programme for new recruits, and training must be given to supervisors to ensure that they are adequately equipped to prepare and carry out on-the-job induction sessions.

Induction therefore affects you in two ways: you are expected to carry it out, and in order to do so effectively you should receive it. If you are expected to carry it out without having received any training or induction yourself, then point this out to your boss. Any competent boss will ensure that matters are swiftly put right.

6 THE SUPERVISOR AS A PROFESSIONAL MANAGER

There are almost as many definitions of a supervisor's job as there are supervisors, but a fairly general one might be: 'To be responsible for the smooth running and production of the goods or services under their control through the resources available to them.'

Of these resources, the most crucial, demanding, frustrating, challenging and rewarding is the people resource. As we have mentioned before, to many people you, as supervisor, are the company. You are involved to a greater or lesser degree in some or all of the following functions: planning, costing, delegation, evaluation, organising, cost control, interviewing, selection, industrial relations, discipline, target setting, counselling, standards, appraisal, training, human relations, communication and coordination. The list could be extended.

All of these functions have something in common: these are the things that managers do. In other words, supervisors are actually managers — although, unfortunately, this is often unrecognised by their own bosses, colleagues, subordinates and, most significantly of all, supervisors themselves.

The first section of this chapter quotes in full an open letter addressed some years ago by The Institute of Supervisory Management to all employers and managers. One of the functions of the institute is to speak up for supervisors, and so in this letter it tried to express what its members felt they could contribute to the national effort.

An open letter

Inflation — parent of anxieties and grandparent of suspicions — has become the bogeyman of Britain, setting us at odds with one another. Not the least damaging of our family feuds is the conflict between the 'two sides' of industry.

How, then, can you, the managers, strengthen unity of purpose in workplaces? We believe that one necessary step is to enlist us, the nation's supervisors. We are strategically placed at the points where management decisions take effect. Yet our jobs are often underestimated.

You 'higher' people see the supervisor's position as 'the bottom rung of the ladder'. In contrast with your wider horizons, ours is a small world, confined to one department or section.

The spearhead

Our first message to you is, therefore: 'Think again about the supervisory outposts. Forget the levels on the organisation chart. Think of the shopfloor as the spearhead of the undertaking — the front line in the battle for efficiency.' A parish council is as necessary as Parliament; our work is as indispensable as finance, marketing or design. Our narrow world provides an ingredient without which no enterprise can thrive: a sense of belonging. Every supervisor is in daily, intimate contact with their people. There is no 'them' and 'us': leaders and led, we are all in the same boat. Our interdependence is self-evident. We are a team — the sort of close-knit unit which has worked effectively throughout history.

To survive, every organisation must be an organism, built up from small cells like ours; the whole cannot be healthy if one cell is cancerous. The supervisor who keeps a cell healthy makes a vital contribution.

'Ask a lot from us'

Our second message to you is, then: 'Ask a lot from us.' We are better placed than anybody else to ask a lot, in turn, from workers. Like good teachers and good chairmen, our art is largely to draw forth enthusiasm from others.

Some of you may say: 'There's precious little enthusiasm about nowadays.' Insofar as this is so, it is, in part at least, attributable to the mistaken idea that you win loyalty by making concessions and conferring benefits. The reverse is true. It is when people contribute something of themselves to an undertaking that they identify with it. This is the constructive aspect of the current demand for participation. The place where people in the small cell can most readily participate is the small cell. Use us, then, to cultivate the good will that finds congenial soil in the small, matey working group. In the nature of things, healthy growth must start at the grass roots. You can't graft it on from above.

Weeding

Our small groups, of course, are not weed-free. They can easily become seed-beds for malignant growths — skiving, backbiting, going slow, and so on. And obviously we have our genuine disputes and grievances to contend with. But fortunately it is in our small world that small problems can often be solved before they grow into big ones. Empower us, then, to weed out unhealthy plants. whenever possible, as soon as they push through the soil.

Our next plea is: 'Take us into your confidence.' We are entitled to some inside knowledge of management policies and purposes. We have learned to be discreet and trustworthy. We are well fitted to pass on to the rank and file as much insight as they can grasp. Our 'in-between' position has accustomed us to the two different languages of management and of the shop floor. We are the natural 'translators' and populariser in these days when people want to know what's what before they consent to be governed — or managed.

Part of the intelligence network

Make us part of your intelligence network, too. We can tell you what really happens on the shop — or office — floor: not only what you want to know, but what you ought to know. We can sift the chaff from the wheat among the workers' ideas and information. We can correct and supplement your shop stewards' lines of communication.

In too many undertakings a 'communication ditch' yawns between us supervisors and our superiors. This divorce between the two branches of management gets less publicity than worker-management disputes, but it can be no less harmful — and can itself cause worker-management strife. So we ask you, the managers, to close the gap between yourselves and us. Make contact with us, informally as well as formally. Get on the same wavelength. Be as close to us as we are to our people. That will bring you close to the shopfloor, too.

Oiling the wheels

Lastly, please think of us, and treat us, as steady fellows who prevent your organisations from dissolving into unmanageable chaos. We are at the friction points, and experience has shown us how to oil the wheels. Emotional forces boil up under the surface in every workplace. We can channel and coordinate these energies, which otherwise might take an anti-managerial turn. You may not want to know about these disturbing influences, but we cannot afford such indifference. We have to cope somehow, and on the whole we 'get by'.

If you appreciated our problems in pulling the chestnuts out of the fire for you, if you went out of your way to back us up, we could do better still. We could show workers more convincingly that their self-interest is by no means diametrically opposed to management's drive for profit. We could be more effective bridge builders, healers of division and creators of unity. In short, if you want to mobilise your rank and file, mobilise us supervisors. We will do the rest.

Not superpeople

We know we are not superpeople. There are weaker brethren and occasional bad eggs. But, even if we are no better than the general run of humanity, we are so placed that, given half a chance, we can do a sound, practical job of leadership. Actually, we may be a bit above average — after all, you chose us for promotion.

We could be an appreciating asset. The more responsibility you give us, the harder you work us — within reason — the more valuable we shall become. Contrast the depreciation of plant in these inflationary days! Just at present, Britain will have to rely very much on the qualities of her people, since she has fallen behind other nations in investment in up-to-date equipment. So, without spending an extra penny, use us to maximise your human resources.

Give us the go-ahead, and we will do our utmost to keep the ship afloat. A crisis is an excellent training ground, because of its real-life urgency. Those of us who have got what it takes will learn a lot in a short time. Those who are inadequate will be shown up and should no doubt be removed as painlessly as possible into less exposed positions. You should, however, distinguish those who merely need more training from those who just can't take it. And in the longer run please see that the right training is given to the right people.

Why you were chosen

The powerful message of that open letter is all too often lost on senior management. You, as a supervisor, are a manager, but you cannot do your job effectively unless the people above you appreciate and publicly acknowledge the fact. Management appoints you, so management should give you their every support. The starting point is the reason you were chosen.

Few managers would claim to have found a foolproof method of selecting supervisors. There are, however, some basic rules. Most well structured organisations are in a position to 'grow their own' — a system which has the advantages that management know what they are getting and all of the employees are motivated by knowing that there is a chance for them to ascend the ladder. If honest information exists on standards of performance and if there is a good system of appraisal, management should have no difficulty in identifying a large number of people who have the potential to be supervisors. With training both before and after promotion, the home-grown supervisor is likely to be a very capable person indeed.

There are a few prerequisites. The prospective supervisor must honestly want to do the job, have some record of success, have the ability to grow, be ultimately acceptable to (i.e., fit in with) any work group, receive basic management training before appointment, know what is expected and understand mutually agreed objectives, help plan his or her own induction programme and know who will help carry this out, and be given the authority and trust that they require if they are to do their job effectively.

The job of management is to spot good supervisors early: too much delay can mean that the person, frustrated, moves on to another company. A good management will not be tempted to appoint supervisors on the 'first available' principle. Often supervisory talent will be spotted when people stand in or substitute during holidays or other short periods: the best fitter or secretary or clerk need not necessarily be the best supervisor.

In the past some organisations seemed to have followed a general policy of appointing shop stewards as supervisors. There is no reason at all why a good staff representative should not make a good supervisor — after all, they are employees as well as staff representatives, have equal status in the selection stakes, and presumably have some leadership qualities as otherwise they would never have become staff representatives in the first place.

What is sometimes in dispute is the reasoning behind such selection. The very worst motive is just to move a bothersome representative so that he or she becomes part of the management structure; the best motive is management's recognition that they are selecting someone who has shown the vital signs of leadership and organisational ability together with the talent of effective communication. It is bad management if a staff representative is automatically excluded from consideration because of his or her union activities: all employees should have equal opportunity, and the selection of supervisors should be chosen as objectively as possible.

Important factors in the management decision are leadership abilities and acceptability to the work group. Leadership ability can be assessed from your activities both in work and outside it. One of management's problems is that it is often difficult for individuals to show compelling evidence of their leadership ability while carrying out their everyday job, and so it is important for management to ascertain what people have achieved outside their work. If you have, shall we say, led a youth club, helped organise social functions, or even done some political canvassing — for whatever party — management will know that you have the ability and urge to influence others. An enlightened management will recognise that this is a more important fact than any technical skills you might have. Of course, you need to have enough technical knowledge to ensure that no one can pull the wool over your eyes, but, as a general rule, if you are acceptable as a leader you will be supported by your group, whereas if you are a technical expert but not acceptable as a leader you are likely to be in deep trouble.

To illustrate this, we can cite a real-life case. An extremely good and hard-working estimator was promoted to be the section leader of his department because his boss had been promoted to become engineering manager. Had management observed this person carefully, they would have seen that he was very much a loner and never took part in any of the section's social activities. He was efficient, but he was quiet and not very creative. When he was told of his impending promotion, he was asked if there were any courses he would like to attend: he asked for one on finance and statistics, subjects very useful for an estimator. At no point during his career had he received any management training.

Soon the new supervisor was adamantly trying to change everyone to conform to his own preferred working method. Also,

90

he was picking for himself all the projects he most enjoyed doing. The team gradually withdrew cooperation, and the work-rate fell; worse still, within a month every single member of the team had applied for transfers. At the 'he goes or we go' stage, a rudely awakened manager stepped in to save the situation — just.

An overseas job cropped up, and the supervisor was sent to do it. During his absence, the right number two was selected, given a short training course and allowed to take over the estimating. On his return from abroad the supervisor was counselled and attended an in-depth management course. Somewhere along the line, realisation dawned, because he is now a very effective manager within that organisation — and in fact he recognises very well the meaning of the word 'acceptability'. He was lucky: quite often the personal traits that give rise to this sort of problem remain with a person for life.

One final point about selection as a supervisor: if you are not training someone to be your successor, it is likely that you are displaying to management and the world at large your own ineligibility for promotion.

Preparation for supervision

It seems inconceivable that anyone would put an untrained operator in charge of expensive equipment, yet often supervisors are thrust into the situation where they are expected to produce results through their handling of people but have been given little or no preparation for handling that element of their job. Of course, you can teach people how to swim by throwing them in at the deep end, but the casualty rate is likely to be high. There are, alas, a few advocates still around of the 'deep end' technique of training supervisors, but fortunately not too many of them.

Many people are promoted as a result of 'situational leadership': this is based on the assumption that the person with the most technical know-how is the best candidate to be the boss. Exactly why the best tool-maker should be the best supervisor of the tool room or the best draughtsman should be put in charge of the studio is a mystery. The best apology is contained in the quotation that 'authority flows from the one who knows'.

Most effective supervisors are familiar with routine and have adequate technical competence, but it is in dealing with people that they are likely to have most to learn. Many managements assume they will somehow acquire this ability through some undefined, almost mystical process; it is to the credit of supervisors that many of them manage not only to survive but also to progress to higher things. Today, when work-group leaders are expected to develop ever-greater leadership skills, this attitude is anachronistic, to put it politely.

Returning to the notion of 'deep end' training, we can note that is often claimed that, the younger one starts, the easier it is, but, just as many people do not learn to swim until they are adults, supervisors are often not given the opportunity to act as a work-group leader until they are well into their mature years, when their personality is well and truly developed and they are likely to be fixed in their ways. Tossing them in at the deep end may therefore have the effect of putting them off wanting to be a supervisor forever.

Whether you are learning to swim or learning to be a supervisor, gradual immersion is the best bet. There are a number of ways by which management can ease you into the duties of your imminent task.

First of all, there is of course standing in for someone else. There are many ways whereby this can come about: the absent person may be sick, away on a course, on holiday or on secondment to other duties; perhaps you may be doing their job for them during overtime. It is important that, when standing in, you ascertain from management the precise extent of your temporary authority and responsibilities, and to make sure that everyone who will be working with or for you is given the same information.

Another management approach is to give you charge of part of a department or area to see how you cope. This is particularly likely if the department is rather on the large side; for example, if there are eighteen people in it, you might be given the control of six of them and the responsibility for a specific part of the overall task of the department.

Giving a prospective supervisor charge of a specific project is preferred by many companies because it is 'low risk/high gain'. It has the advantage to management that they can monitor your performance in terms of your interaction with other people when you are in the situation of leading them. Also, more often than not, it means that the project is done sooner rather than later, which can be a good thing in itself. From leading a project you can gain valuable experience in report writing, fact finding and so on.

Progressive delegation is an important way in which supervisors can train their successors. Certain responsibilities and authority are handed over to the potential successor gradually, until he or she is promoted to take charge of a specific area. It is important that this is true delegation, and not just a matter of turning the potential successor into a glorified message carrier: true delegation means not only giving people extra responsibility but also the relevant amount of authority to enable them to fulfil that responsibility.

The term 'the Grand Tour' is sometimes used to describe a collection of the methods described above. If you suspect that this will be a question of just tagging along behind your departmental head, protest: it will be boring for you and irritating for your boss, who will tend to view you as a nuisance who is always getting in the way — hardly the most propitious attitude if you are to be recommended for promotion! However, at its best the Grand Tour can be very valuable, giving you experience in a number of interrelated departments.

One final point on all these methods is that everyone concerned should have been notified before you were brought in on the act. There is nothing worse when you are trying to find your feet than to be confronted by either indifference or outright hostility simply because other people involved have not been told that you — at least temporarily — are in charge.

Outside training

Preparation within the company is obviously of inestimable value, but formal training off the job can be of considerable use as well to the prospective supervisor. Of course, experience and ability are essential requirements at any level of management, but formal training is important, too. There are many approaches, but some form of regular, structured and preferably participative and practical training should be programmed into every supervisor's busy working life.

As we saw, management will take into account the fact that the person concerned has bothered to attend relevant courses; if the person has spent his or her own time and money bettering their own ability, this too can be nothing but a good sign. There are many outside training courses a company can send people to. The biggest problem there is likely to be is in organising other people around the person's absence, especially on the longer courses and especially if the person is employed in rotating shift work. This problem can, however, be overcome with the help of good management and flexible training organisations.

One of the old favourites, and none the less effective for that, is the NEBSS (National Examinations Board for Supervisory Studies) course usually run by local technical colleges. TWI courses are usually done by day-release, or they can be run in-house by arrangement, and NEBSS courses can be done by day-release or in the evenings. TWI courses do not involve any examinations, and are essentially for job instruction — they provide a basic, short opening course. Various City-and-Guilds-type courses are an option, and these can be a great help in making middle-aged brains regain the greater flexibility of youth. Two of the most effective courses now becoming available nationally (and, indeed, internationally) are the ISM (Institute of Supervisory Management) Certificate and Diploma courses; both last for a year, and they can be organised for day-release, evenings or even in-house. They are not examination courses, but are run on a continuous-assessment basis whereby shortcomings are spotted and corrected in the early stages. This system allows a person's progress to be continually monitored, the aim being to bring about a minimum improvement in performance over eight or ten 'modules' directed at the practical needs of a supervisor. Interestingly, some universities are currently looking at this system as a perhaps more realistic way of educating people than simply grooming them for a final examination.

If you are lucky, the training methods used in your organisation will combine inside, on-the-job and off-the-job methods. If you are sent to external courses it can help to broaden your horizons, develop your self-confidence and make you realise that you are not alone in facing the challenges of your particular type of job. Because a mixed bag of talents is represented among the other people on the course, you can get a fuller insight into the way you operate and make you test your preconceptions 'away from home'.

Leadership

Ask any manager what he or she reckons are the qualities a good supervisor should have and you are likely to receive some or all

of the following replies:
- resilience
- courage
- dependability
- integrity
- forcefulness
- decisiveness
- dedication
- good judgement
- understanding
- ambition
- a sense of humour

You would get the same sort of answers if you asked any given group of people: 'What qualities constitute a good leader?' The trouble is, few of us — yourself excepted, of course — are such paragons that we display all, or even most of, these qualities, and yet organisations require a lot of supervisors. Moreover, there are certain problems of meaning in the list of qualities; for example, does 'dependable' mean quite the same as 'reliable'? Yet the method of assessing prospective supervisors in terms of their perceived qualities is still widely prevalent.

Even supposing agreement can be reached on definitions, there is still the hurdle of subjectivity. If you attempt to decide whether someone is suitable for promotion by comparing the person's character with a preordained list of desirable qualities you are necessarily basing your judgement on wholly subjective grounds. Should more than one person be involved in making the choice there is every possibility that they will disagree on the precise qualities the candidate does or does not possess. This is simply because in assessing people in this way you are calling for one person's opinion about another — which is to say that the final judgement will be subjective rather than objective.

If people cannot be trained to be something, they most certainly can be trained to do something. This is a functional rather than an idealistic approach to the training of managers, supervisors included: elsewhere I have described this concept as Action-centred Leadership (*see*, for instance, a companion volume to this book, *The Action-centred Leader*). This simply means what it says: leadership centred on the action of the leader — that is, on what the leader does, rather than the type of person the leader is or should be.

There are three key areas to be considered if you are to be trained as an effective supervisor, or if you are in the process of training your successor. These can be summed up as

- achieve task
- develop individuals
- build team

It is your job as a leader to see that you meet these three basic needs. This method of developing and improving leadership applies not just to new supervisors but also to experienced ones.

A team exists because its purpose or task cannot be achieved by one person alone. It is because of this common purpose that a team is distinguishable from a random crowd. The members of the team feel a strong need to accomplish the task, and they have to feel that their leader will enable them to do so. They want to feel that the leader can plan, organise and control effectively, that he or she knows what the team is trying to achieve, and that the team's efforts are effectively directed towards a relevant goal.

However well and humanely they are treated by their leader, and however much they may like him or her as a person, if the team members do not have this faith in their leader, and if it becomes evident that the team is not achieving its task, they will become demoralised and frustrated. So achieving the task is an important part of your role as a supervisor.

What about development of the individual? Every team member has individual needs. They need to know what is expected of them, to feel that they are making a significant and worthwhile contribution to the task, and to receive adequate recognition for this. They need to know that the job is demanding the best of them, that their abilities are not underused, that they have responsibility to match their capability, that they are being stretched, challenged and enabled to grow in stature psychologically, and that they can look back and think: 'A year ago I couldn't do this, but I can now!' In addition, they need to feel that they belong to a team, that they are accepted and valued members, and that they count. Occasionally they may require help or counselling about some problem which is new to them and therefore possibly unnerving through its unfamiliarity.

That is quite a collection of needs, but all of these — and more — are likely to be felt by every member of your team, and it is your job to satisfy those needs. Nobody ever said being a supervisor was easy! Unless your team members' needs are met they may, as it were, withdraw from the group: they will be at work, but not really working.

The third aspect of your leadership involves building your team. Any group develops its own personality, which is quite distinct from those of its members. This can often be apparent when the behaviour of an individual is quite different to the behaviour of the group as a whole. This is something which trade unions understand very well, and something which you would do well to learn.

A group has the power to set its own standards of behaviour and performance, and to impose them even when they are contrary to the interests of individuals and the organisation. It is part of your job to gain the acceptance of your group so that you can direct their energies constructively. Remember, the energies of any group rarely lie dormant, doing nothing, so it is vital that they be channelled towards constructive ends. You must think about — and, more important, actually do — things that result in the members of your team having a loyalty to each other and to the team as a whole, a pride in belonging, a desire to work together as a team, and an acceptance of the standards you suggest, which, once accepted, will maintain themselves. In short, what you must do is achieve and maintain morale in your team.

Conflict will certainly arise within the team, but you can put this to effective use. Do not allow it to become disruptive or simply stifle it; instead, utilise it for the creativity and the ideas it can generate.

There is a synergistic effect between each of these three aspects of leadership we have been discussing. Graphically, it is represented in the diagram on page 7. It is not by accident that the three circles overlap: the three key areas interact. For example, it is essential for the group to feel they are achieving something in the task if group morale and individual satisfaction are to be high. Likewise, if the group is riven by internal dissensions and jealousies, its performance suffers, as does the degree of individual satisfaction.

It is important for you as a leader to take action to ensure the best possible results in all three areas, but in real life it is hardly practicable to give equal attention to each of the three. There will always be instances when you have to devote all your energies to the task (to meet a deadline, for example), because the task has priority at the the time: temporarily, the other two areas must suffer. This is reasonable, and most thinking people are prepared to accept it — so long as you show you are aware of your necessary neglect of the other two areas, and, at the earliest possible opportunity, put a little extra effort into them.

Some supervisors consistently ignore or pay little attention to specific areas of need. There is the familiar 'task-oriented' supervisor who habitually ignores people problems, especially those involving individuals. These supervisors are usually highly efficient, think ahead, and give clear instructions which they expect to be obeyed promptly, but they are just not interested in people as people. Their philosophy tends to be: 'People are paid to come here to do a job. They are not asked to bring their problems or personal difficulties with them. I'm not interested in excuses — just results!' In the short term, this sort of ruthlessly efficient supervisor does indeed get results, but usually the results are fairly poor in the longer term. If only the potential of the individual team members was harnessed more effectively, the results achieved in the longer term would be getting better and better, not worse and worse.

You can see this if you think about the 'develop individuals' circle in the diagram being blacked out: a bite is taken out of each of the other two. If you are failing to develop the people in your team, the needs of the task are not being met and nor is group morale as high as it could be.

Another bad hat — if for the best of moral reasons — is the 'people-oriented' supervisor. Their philosophy is: "If you treat people right they'll work without any pushing.' True — but not the whole truth. It is not so much a problem of the supervisor failing to achieve to results: it is more that, whenever he or she sees a conflict between the demands of the task and the needs of the individual, the latter is the factor that gets the support. This approach is perhaps best illustrated by a repair-shop manager who once remarked to a staggered audience: 'We don't repair many engines here, but we have a happy shop.' Supervisors like this usually make a point of knowing the personal backgrounds of all their people and following the progress of their families, their illnesses, their holiday adventures, their children's educational successes and failures ... Such supervisors usually attract great loyalty from the members of their team (something which should never be discounted), but there is always a vague sense of unease among the group members, because they know that they are not being as successful as they could be, or even should be: they are failing to achieve. Again, think about the 'achieve task' circle in the diagram being blacked out, and look at the effects on the other two. If you are totally people-oriented, individuals will know that they are not being stretched and will turn their energies in other directions, some of which will not be in the organisation's interests, or even their own.

It is important, therefore, that your approach be a balanced one if you are to be an effective leader. You do not need to be a 'born' leader in order to be an effective one: all you need to do is think about these three simple areas of your job in terms of your obligations both to your organisation and to your team members, and the rest will follow easily.

The structure of the organisation

What effect does the structure of your organisation have on the nature and effectiveness of your leadership?

Companies often employ people specially to help with task functions — for example, coping with technical problems, maintaining quality standards and deciding work priorities. They may handle team functions, like arranging holiday cover, implementing safety procedures and making sure that communication is good. They will commonly deal with individual functions such as selection, grievance, discipline and counselling interviews and decisions, the following up of absenteeism, and induction training. These 'specialists' include advisory staff such as training officers, quality inspectors, rate fixers and safety officers. Shop stewards, charge hands and the supervisor's boss may also be involved.

The trouble is, the more these functions are divided up, the more your team members are likely to be confused about who is their leader. It is therefore vital to the effectiveness of any supervisor as a leader that as many of these responsibilities as possible should remain in the supervisor's domain, although he or she may choose to delegate them to others.

When you contemplate what is needed from you as a leader to meet the requirements of the three circles (see page 7) — in terms of task, team and individuals — you can see why it is difficult for any leader to lead effectively a team of more than fifteen people. As far as possible, too, those people should always report to the same boss, and not to a selection of bosses according to shift pattern.

Action-Centred Leadership, a simple but practical method of leadership, has been adopted by many companies and thousands of managers and supervisors have received training in it. In almost all cases, the companies themselves have reported improvements in the way that their supervisors have, through realising that they are managers, begun to do the job of actually managing, helped achievement of the task, increased team work and given greater satisfaction to the individual members of their team.

Never forget that you are first and foremost a leader. It is possible that the structure of the organisation you work for will inhibit your expression of your leadership — in which case it is up to you to try to alter that structure, initially by approaching your own direct boss and pointing up the problem. If you get no useful response — well, there are other companies who would no doubt be glad of your services, especially because you have shown the initiative to try to do something about what is obviously a seriously flawed company structure. Most likely, though, your boss will realise the difficulty, and your life as a supervisor will become much easier as you become the leader you ought to be.

7 INDUSTRIAL RELATIONS

Industrial relations have attracted more comment from politicians and laypeople than any other aspect of our industrial life. The whole matter has been blown up out of all proportion, because its origins are very simple: industrial relations are just human relations which happen to be at the place of work. This is true whether or not there is trade-union representation, but for the sake of this chapter we shall assume that your organisation recognises a union or unions, and that the staff representatives are union shop stewards. Unfortunately, just as the term 'industrial relations' has become for many people a synonym for confrontation, so has the label 'shop steward' become identified with the arbiters or even instigators of such confrontation.

Of course, it would be silly to pretend that confrontation does not exist, or that all shop stewards are blameless. In this chapter we hope to put industrial relations in perspective and to give you some guidance on the basics. Although you cannot hope to find all the answers here, perhaps you will find enough to help you contain many industrial-relations problems at their rightful level — that is, between you and your shop steward. The last thing you want is for any problem to escalate so that it affects — adversely — the organisation as a whole.

Relationships with trade unions obviously vary from company to company, and so some of the ideas in this chapter will be more relevant to you than others. Overall, however, it is to be hoped that they constitute a coherent and productive approach to the matter of industrial relations.

It is worth remembering that, in your aim to be an effective supervisor, the shop steward can be your best friend: the vast majority of shop stewards are not the bogeymen depicted in the tabloid press, but people who want to make life easier for everyone in the working group, including you. This is why some managements not only recognise but positively encourage unions. Here is an example of the statement of an enlightened company to its new employees on the matter of union membership:

> The management believes that it is in the interests of employees
> and of the company that employees should be members of the
> appropriate trade union. Union membership is not a condition
> of employment, but the company recommends its employees
> to join and to maintain membership of an appropriate union
> so that relationships between the company and the union can
> be on a fully representative and authoritative basis.

In an organisation which is already unionised it may seem
depressingly difficult to change existing practices and attitudes
— assuming, as one usually can, that there is room for
improvement in the organisation's industrial relations. In an
organisation that has not had previous dealings with unions, and
which is now faced by the fact that employees wish to become
union members, the problem lies in what to do about it and when.
Both situations call for clear and realistic thinking about the
respective roles of management and unions and the determination
to develop policies and procedures that will result in constructive
management-union relations.

Of course, much of this may seem rather rarefied to the average
supervisor: after all, it is hardly your decision as to whether or
not the company recognises unions. However, to the members
of your team, you are the management — and certainly you should
consider yourself as a manager. The success or otherwise of
industrial relations as practised at your departmental level will
affect the entire organisation.

You may well be a union member yourself, in which case you
will recognise the valuable role that unions can play in industrial
relations. The growth of the white-collar unions still tends to be
regarded by many managers with surprise and possibly some
dismay. In fact, the reduction in the differentials between
shopfloor employees and office ones, the marked change in the
ratio between staff and manual workers, the tendency towards
the greater concentration in one place of staff employees and the
general increase in size and complexity of industrial, commercial
and public-service undertakings have all contributed to the
inevitability of the growth of white-collar unions. By the early
1980s the membership of white-collar unions exceeded that of
blue-collar unions, and nowadays the big growth area is among
senior employees up to executive level.

Whether your team members are in a blue-collar or a white-collar union, your aim should be to ensure that industrial relations are good. It is all too easy to blame the unions when they break down, but in fact there is almost always fault to be found on both sides. As a supervisor you have the power to make sure that industrial relations remain good in your own area. Success in this is one of the signs of an effective leader.

Management attitudes towards trade unions

Do we need trade unions? The range of opinions among managers varies widely, but they can be boiled down into two prime categories.

On the one hand you have those who think that industry would run very much better if there were no unions and if managers were left to get on with it by themselves. Managers who hold this view generally believe that the right thing to do is to oppose the unions, or at any rate actively to discourage them. The view is generally to be found among managers who have up 'til now worked in a non-union environment and who believe the horror stories about the unions they read in the popular press. Managers of this type tend to think of all the individuals in their organisation as members of a team, all with the same clearly defined common purpose: if they are not pulling together, well, they jolly well ought to be. Such managers, no matter how hard they try to keep up to date with what they think or do about industrial relations, at heart may resent the fact that unions exist.

The other side of the coin are managers who take a positive attitude. Not only do they accept the fact that unions exist, they believe that unions have an important role to perform and that it is up to everyone in management to take the initiative and make sure that the unions are indeed performing that role.

People who take this positive attitude recognise that conflict between management and unions is as likely but no more likely than conflict between different sections of management — for example, between sales executives who are trying to satisfy customers and production executives who are in the midst of installing new machinery. However, having identified and accepted areas in which conflict might arise, good managers are able to agree with the unions' procedures for the orderly and swift resolution of disputes and grievances, and are also better placed to eliminate or reduce conflict in all those areas where it can be avoided — of which there are many.

The old cliché has it that there are 'two sides' in industry, and so it is worth a few lines to squash the idea. In the sense that they have different roles to play and different functions to perform, management and unions do indeed constitute 'two sides'. However, in the sense that they have a common interest in the prosperity of industry, there is only a single side. Although it is in the interest of both management and unions that industry should prosper and grow, there are differences in opinion about how the benefits of growth and development should be shared, and there may very well be different ideas as to how growth and prosperity can best be promoted. Essentially, the role of the unions is to look after the interests of their members in both the short and the long term, while management has to think not only about the welfare of employees but also about the interests of shareholders and customers. There is likely to be a clash when it comes to deciding about who gets what share of the cake, but the important thing is that both unions and management are essentially dedicated to increasing the size of the cake. If the objectives of the organisation and the individuals within it are to be achieved, management and unions need to cooperate.

All too often, both management and unions forget this. You, as a supervisor, are well placed to remind both of them of the fact.

Employees' attitudes towards trade unions

There is much that could be said on the subject of people's reasons for joining trade unions, but it is enough to note that for well over half a century collective bargaining has been the accepted method of determining wages and conditions. Today, around three-quarters of the UK workforce is covered by collective agreements between employers (or their federations) and unions. In joining a union an employee is simply becoming part of a system that is completely accepted by most employers as well as by the state. The system may not be perfect, but a better one has yet to be found.

One of the main reasons why people join a union is job security.

Mergers, takeovers and closures having become commonplace, employees see membership of a trade union as a means of safeguarding their interests. Even in an organisation where management-employee relations are good and the conditions of employment are above average, people recognise, quite rightly, that there are economic forces over which their managements have no control. Those employees desire protection, and who could blame them?

Younger employees have a different conception of loyalty from that of their elders: they may be equally loyal, but in a rather different way. They are more questioning, more aware, and keener to be involved in the processes that determine their terms and conditions. One way of meeting this need is for them to join a trade union.

For senior people, in technical and managerial roles, union membership gives a greater influence over the organisation's affairs. Too often senior employees are left out of the picture, the sole dialogue within the organisation seeming to take place between the apex and the base. Union membership allows these senior people to find out what is happening, rather than wait for the news to percolate upwards from the base. And, of course, in the years leading up to retirement, a union can be particularly effective in protecting the individual's rights.

The role and function of trade unions

The basic function of a trade union is to represent its members. Through either in-house representatives or full-time union officials, the unions provide a means for a collective expression of views, reactions and requirements both to the managements of individual organisations and to employers' associations.

In all but the smallest organisations, the practical arguments in favour of having a representative system are overwhelmingly strong. With the best will in the world, management cannot hope to get a true picture of employee attitudes and aspirations if it relies on individual contacts and consultations. A representative system helps to ensure that employees' interests are taken into account — something which may well be a major factor in the satisfactory achievement of change. When employees' interests clash with those of management, a representative system is the only way whereby justice can not only be done but be seen to be done.

Many people argue that a representative system can be organised just as well without union involvement. Certainly it can be tried, and it frequently is — often as a short-sighted defensive measure by managements who want to keep the unions out at all costs — but there is overwhelming evidence that any non-union representative system such as a staff association after a while ceases to have any real effectiveness. The reason is that such systems lack the independence of unionised representation, so that management-employee dialogues lose any edge and purpose. Another point is that a staff association may be a lot less constructive than a union: it has to prove itself if it is to forestall employees from joining a union, and so it may be that much more demanding simply in order to justify its own existence.

There is a tendency to think of unions as being concerned only with securing higher wages and better conditions of employment. Clearly these are main objectives of any trade union, but they are also manifestations of something much more fundamental: a concern for the dignity and self-respect of the individual. Over the years, the unions have done a great deal to improve the physical conditions of people's work: their activities have benefited industrial health and safety. Unions have also contributed much to greater efficiency, higher productivity and the better use of people.

In a wider context, unions, as representatives of the workforce, are involved in many aspects of national and regional life, from local arts associations to the formulation of Government policies. Some politicians are eager to try to reduce the role of unions in national and economic matters, but this is wishful and rather counterproductive thinking: if the economy is to prosper, then both management and employees must be deeply involved, and the most effective way of ensuring that employees are involved is that they be represented by a trade union.

Of course, every barrel has a rotten apple, but even if the shop steward you have to deal with is difficult and argumentative, and seems to be athirst for confrontation, bear in mind that that person is the exception. The unions have a valuable role to play in achieving the objectives of your team, your organisation and industry as a whole.

Recognition and membership

Wise managers accept that, once they have recognised unions, there are a number of practical things they can do to create and maintain good relations.

In a situation where previously there has been no union presence but where there are the first signs of union activity or even where the union is asking for recognition, things can be delicate, to put it mildly. It is hard to blame managers for wanting to put off having to deal with unions for as long as possible, particularly if they feel that they have always got on perfectly well without them in the past. At the same time, it is foolish for any manager to ignore the fact that collective bargaining is widely accepted as the normal method of determining employees' terms and conditions, or to suppose that at some point there will not be a move towards union representation among employees. If employers accept the inevitability of the eventual recognition of unions, they should act positively and constructively when the subject is first mooted among their employees. In organisations where management-union relations are poor, this is often because managers have failed to influence and guide the relationship when it was in its infancy. Of course, the management-union relationship imposes constraints on both sides, but if properly tackled those very constraints can and should be productive. Obviously you cannot determine your organisation's attitudes towards union recognition — that is something for senior management — but, once the recognition has been granted, you can do a lot to make sure that the further relations are constructive ones.

Usually management is aware when a union is first starting to recruit within the organisation. The first formal approach is likely to come from a full-time official of the union, who will either claim bargaining rights or ask for the recognition of shop stewards (fathers-of-chapel, etc.), or both. The most sensible response is, as quickly as possible, to arrange a meeting with the union official; it is not a good plan for management to make any statements on the subject to employees before this meeting, but all levels of management should be kept informed of what is going on.

At the meeting with the union official, management should establish as precisely as possible exactly which sections of the workforce the union claims to represent. Once that is clear, it is possible to assess a realistic figure for the percentage of employees who have already joined the union, and at the same time agreement can be reached as to how high this percentage should be if the management is formally to recognise the union. (Of course, the percentage figure may already have been reached.) At this stage it is reasonable to talk in terms of majority or substantial support for the union (see below); this could be done by carrying out a ballot or a survey of employees' attitudes.

Pending full recognition, some managements grant representational as opposed to full bargaining rights; that is, they give the union the right to represent a member who has an individual grievance, but they do not concede to the union the right to negotiate wages or conditions of service. Agreeing representational rights is a good idea only if it is anticipated that full recognition is on the way.

If management is satisfied that it is dealing with the most appropriate union (or that the union is itself adequate, or there is no viable alternative) and if the percentage of union members is too low to justify automatic recognition but nevertheless sufficient to indicate substantial interest in union recognition (i.e., about 20-25 per cent), the most effective first steps management can take are as follows:

- agree with the unions times and facilities for recruiting members at the place of work
- prepare a brief formal statement referring to the discussions with the union, indicating that recognition will depend on additional or majority support
- explain the policy to all members of management, and discuss it fully: not everyone will agree with the policy, but at least they should understand and support it
- issue a formal statement to all employees and explain it to them verbally — if there is a consultative committee it should be discussed there, too

Assessing the moment at which recognition should be granted is not an easy matter. Having indicated at the outset to the union that a majority of the employees concerned should be in the union, some managers argue from experience that it is better to settle for a lower percentage. If a union is making inroads into the workforce, there will be a few activists, a few who are strongly anti-union, and a large band of 'don't knows'. Naturally, the activists work away at the apathetic majority, and union membership goes up to around the 30-40 per cent mark, where it tends to slow up and sometimes to stick. This can be a dangerous time, because management insistence on a 51 per cent membership before recognition is granted can cause needless militancy and antagonism; also, haggling acrimoniously over the precise number of people in the union is hardly the best foundation to lay for future management-union cooperation. If, by contrast, management recognises the union sooner rather than later, it is in a much stronger position to get the terms it wants in the formal recognition and procedural agreements. An additional benefit is that, if there is a long hang-fire period when support for one union is at the 30-40 per cent level, a different union may start recruiting, which is the last thing management wants: a single union can be of immense benefit to an organisation, but dealing with a plurality can be tremendously time-wasting. Experience has shown that, after recognition has been agreed and employees learn that a union has negotiating rights, membership increases significantly — especially if management plays its part in encouraging employees to join the union.

Once management has decided on recognition in principle, a second and even more vital stage in the process begins. This consists of discussing and agreeing with the union(s) all those matters that provide the framework for industrial relations within the organisation, as determined in the recognition and procedural agreements. These topics should include:

- the responsibilities of union representatives, and the facilities (including time off) allowed to them to carry out those responsibilities
- the provision of written credentials for union representatives
- a clear and workable procedure for settling issues and grievances
- a carefully thought out disciplinary procedure

All of this requires a lot of hard work and a great deal of talking, but the time is well spent. Managements that allow themselves to be rushed into half-baked recognition and procedure agreements miss a golden opportunity to get industrial relations within their organisations off on the right foot. While these agreements should obviously be as comprehensive and precise as possible, it is in fact the tone and spirit of the discussions leading

109

up to them being signed that can determine the long-term future of industrial relations within the organisation.

If industrial relations are to be constructive, they depend on maximum participation by union members in the system of collective representation and negotiation. Clearly individuals who do not wish to join a union should be free to opt out, but there is no reason why management should not show that it approves of the fact that its employees are joining an appropriate recognised union and playing a part in its activities. It is perfectly permissible for managements to encourage employees to join recognised unions; managers who disagree on this, saying that recruitment is the unions' job rather than the management's, are ignoring a few salient points:

- If all or the majority of employes in the bargaining unit are members of the union, there is a better chance that people of the right calibre will emerge as union representatives. By the 'right calibre' we do not mean management toadies — they serve the interests of nobody. Good shop stewards are people who understand the respective roles of management and unions and can effectively represent the real views of the majority of their fellow employees.
- Union officials and shop stewards with a high percentage membership behind them are less likely to feel that they have to 'play to the gallery'. If their membership is low, on the other hand, they may have difficulty in making agreements stick because they do not have the authority to carry through their part of the bargain.
- Low or fluctuating membership and ineffective or unpopular representation may lead to proliferation of the number of unions involved in the organisation. Full and active membership of a few recognised unions makes for stability.

In short, the fewer union representatives management has to deal with and the more influential those representatives are, the better for all concerned: less time is consumed by endless meetings with people who have different interests, inter-union bickering is minimised, representatives feel sure of their position and so can develop a good and useful relationship with management, employees are secure that all of their interests are being represented equally ... the list could go on.

What about your own membership of a union?

While managements often adopt a positive attitude towards the unionisation of manual and office workers, they sometimes find it harder to accept that their supervisors and managers likewise want to become members of a union — often because they feel that the act of joining up is in some way disloyal. As we know, supervisors are part of the management team, but at the same time they may also feel a need for collective representation in matters such as pay, promotion, status and authority. This is felt particularly when differentials between them and the people they supervise are eroded, or when there is talk of changes in the organisation which are likely to create redundancies or reduce promotion prospects. Perhaps you feel that you are unaware of all the undercurrents of activity within the company: if your subordinates have so much influence through their union membership, why shouldn't you have a slice of the action, too?

Supervisors promoted from the shop floor often stay in the union to which they already belong. Many remain members in name only: if they are anything more than this, and carry on as members of the same branch, represented by the same shop steward, they cannot perform their job as supervisors properly. It is therefore a good idea to ensure that you are not a member of the same branch or section as the people whom you supervise, and that the shop steward whose job it is to represent you is not someone over whom you have supervisory responsibilities. If you do not tackle these points for yourself, there is every chance that management will intervene with your union and do it for you. A number of unions recognise these concerns, and have special sections for supervisors.

Shop stewards

The influence and consequent importance of the shop steward have grown with the increase in the negotiating power of the work group. Plant bargaining, which today often takes the form of self-financing productivity, has in many cases put the shop steward very much in the lead position, the full- time union official, who has many other duties, simply not having the time to get involved in every local negotiation.

New techniques and technologies and legislation on things like health and safety require new skills and greater flexibility among employees, so plant-level bargaining and consultation have become more important than ever before. It is therefore necessary for organisations to have effective and responsible shop stewards who understand the issues at stake, can present a case logically and reasonably, and report back to their members clearly and reasonably.

The job of a shop steward is not an easy one: the steward has to double up the roles of employee and elected representative, while at the same time being the visible face of the union to its members. In dealing with an individual grievance, the steward has the task of acting in the interests not only of that individual but also of the majority.

It is important that neither stewards nor management should see the role of the shop steward only in terms of negotiation and the settlement of grievances: stewards must be recognised as representatives of their members in all of the matters that affect them. Management should keep stewards well informed of plans and future developments and, whenever appropriate, should make a point of consulting them.

Effective shop stewards can make an enormous difference to the efficiency, productivity and morale of an organisation. What can management — from chairman to supervisor — do to influence the type and quality of the men and women elected to be shop stewards and to make sure that they are properly equipped to carry out the task? The first thing managers can do is to take a positive attitude towards unions in general, so that no one thinks that becoming a shop steward is likely to affect their career prospects. Otherwise, there are four main areas in which management as a whole can act:

- qualifications and elections
- recognition
- facilities
- training

Let us look at these four in turn.

Qualifications and elections

At the outset, management should discuss with the union(s) the minimum qualifications, in terms of career within the organisation and duration of membership of the union, that a shop steward should have: it might be that, unless people had been with the company for a year and members of the union for six months, they are not eligible for election. Managements should take more care than they often do when discussing these points.

Another topic of discussion should be the number of shop stewards to be elected and the areas or groups which they will represent. Also, if it can be arranged, it should be agreed that elections should be conducted outside the factory or office, so that maximum employee participation is encouraged. High polls and the widest possible interest can also be encouraged if election dates and details are given publicity on notice-boards. However you go about it, make sure that all the members of your team are fully aware of the fact that there is an upcoming chance for them to vote for the representative of their choice. At the same time, make sure you do not attempt in any way to influence their selection: for a variety of reasons, this is the worst possible thing you could do.

Recognition of shop stewards

Stewards should have written credentials issued jointly by their management and their union: these should be signed by a senior member of management, the appropriate union official, and by the steward. They should state clearly the steward's rights and responsibilities and be specific about such topics as the period of office for which the steward has been elected, the department or section which the steward has been elected to represent, the agreements and rules to which the steward has undertaken to agree, and the steward's rights and responsibilities.

The purpose of written credentials is not just to acknowledge that a particular individual has been elected: they also show that management recognises that the job of the steward is an important and responsible one; also, they are a useful way of encouraging the ablest people to stand for election.

Sometimes unions are not willing to give sanction to the issuing of joint credentials. In such a case, management should supply stewards with a formal letter acknowledging their election and assuring the person that management will give all the support that they reasonably can (the union should of course be consulted about the content of such letters). Management has the power, in practice, to withhold or withdraw such letters or written credentials, but this should occur only if there are clear-cut and visibly justifiable reasons for so doing.

On election, stewards should be given copies of all the relevant

113

agreements, rules and schemes (a particularly important document is the one outlining the negotiating procedure), together with any necessary verbal explanation. In addition, a senior manager should always hold an interview with a newly elected shop steward if for no other reason (and there should be plenty) than that the meeting indicates the importance which the company attaches to the job of being a shop steward.

Finally, management's recognition of shop stewards affects you, the supervisor. You must make a point of acknowledging the appointment of a new supervisor in your department, and must make a point of arranging a meeting at which the two of you can discuss how best you can cooperate. For example, you might set up a system whereby the two of you have brief but frequent discussions of departmental developments.

Facilities for shop stewards

By law, shop stewards must continue to receive average earnings while carrying out their industrial-relations functions within the company. Management and unions should agree beforehand the circumstances in which shop stewards can leave their normal job in order to carry out their representational duties. Obviously stewards should first ask permission from their supervisor; equally obviously, such permission should be granted in all but the most exceptional circumstances.

Training

Defining the rights and responsibilities of shop stewards and giving them copies of all the relevant agreements is easy enough, but making sure they understand these documents is quite another. This is where formal training becomes important. Any management needs to make sure that the organisation's shop stewards are fully trained as to their role, the aims, policies and organisation of the union to which they belong, the policies and other matters relating to the organisation, the agreements that have been established between the organisation and the union, the skills required for the job, and anything that is likely to occur in the overlap of interests between the organisation and the union.

Both managements and unions are becoming increasingly aware of the need for training shop stewards, and it is a joint management-union responsibility to ensure that such training is provided. The employer's duty is to pay the new shop steward at normal levels for any time he or she might have to take off normal work in order to undergo the training.

Who actually carries out the training is as important as seeing that it is in fact done. An in-company or in-service training course can cover all the various facets described above. However, since the idea of supervisors having a hand in the training of their own shop stewards is still viewed with suspicion in many quarters, it is sometimes best if the job is tackled by a third party, such as the Industrial Society, which can advise on the content of the course, take some of the sessions and, as it were, act as a neutral chairman.

8 HEALTH AND SAFETY AT WORK

In terms of health and safety at work, there are, at the time of writing, various important Acts of Parliament about which every supervisor should have a general knowledge. Among these are the Factories Act 1961, the Offices, Shops and Railway Premises Act 1963, the Health and Safety at Work Act 1974, the Safety Representatives and Safety Committees Act 1978, and the Health and Safety (First Aid Regulations) Act 1981. The most important of these is the Health and Safety at Work Act.

There are various publications that spell out all the implications of all these various Acts — and so in this chapter we shall look at the subject only insofar as it is likely to affect your job as a supervisor.

Safe working methods

None of us would deny the need for accident prevention at work, but probably no two people would have exactly the same attitude to the problem, or the same means of approaching it. Let us consider some of the attitudes that are current.

Some managers and supervisors sincerely believe that people should not be coddled — that they will learn best if they learn the hard way. You can imagine such a person, while walking through their section, seeing a chunk of wood on the floor and thinking: 'I'll bet some silly ass will trip over that before the day is out. Still, it'll probably teach him to look where he's going and watch out in future.' Later, one can imagine the manager or supervisor saying to someone who has suffered a minor injury because of that lump of wood: 'Well, I told you so. If you do daft things it serves you right. If you'd only think while you were on the job you wouldn't get hurt.' The temptation to tell people that, if only they did such and such, they would not get hurt seems to be fairly common. Of course, the person might be dead because

116

of the accident, in which case it is a little late to say 'I told you so'.

Then again, there are some supervisors who think that production is the only concern: for them, the job comes first, last and all the time. They feel that they need not be too concerned about the risk of an accident, and that the dangers everyone else worries about may never really cause someone to be hurt. They accept small risks, justifying them on the basis that production must be kept up. You can imagine such a supervisor saying: 'Don't worry — it may never happen. Let's concentrate on getting the job done.' The trouble here is that, although a risk may indeed be slight, if it happens it happens 100 per cent — something appreciated by anyone who has suffered as a result of an industrial accident.

Supervisors who have seen a serious accident in their section tend to put safety above everything else. No job can start until the supervisor has pondered over whether there is a slightest risk of someone being injured. Such supervisors preach the doctrine of safety to such a degree that people get tired of hearing about it and suspect that, at any moment, they are likely to be tapped on the shoulder and told they are doing something dangerous; in short, they get jittery. This hardly helps their work, and in fact is likely to lead to a higher level of accidents.

So far we have considered three types of supervisors:

- the 'let 'em learn' type
- the 'production first, last and all the time' type
- the 'safety before everything' type

As we have seen, all three types are risking the health and even the lives of the people who work for them.

Turning for a moment to your own section, is it possible that a hazard has already started to form? A loosening stair-rod, a flickering light on a landing, a loose screw in an electrical fitting, a worker who has developed the habit of popping things into a gangway 'just for a moment' ... Hazards often come into existence slowly and surreptitiously: they start off in a small way, grow gradually, and without anyone realising it develop until a nasty accident becomes almost inevitable.

Think of the effect on the organisation if an accident occurs: morale and production plummet and there is a perhaps considerable financial loss. From the victim's point of view, there is suffering, potential loss of earnings, deleterious effects on his or her dependants, and, in the long term, the possibility of being unable to do the same job, or any other, ever again.

The normal tendency is to think only of the major dangers, but let us consider the smaller ones as well, because small dangers, by going undetected, become large ones. Safety, you have to accept, is a normal part of your job. Without being paranoid on the subject, you have to be alert to the possibility of all dangers, whether large or small. The need for accident prevention is best seen if we consider the costs of injuries from various angles.

From the victim's point of view, social insurance benefits and any form of compensation and relief can never fully make good for the financial losses arising from an accident. On purely humanitarian grounds, therefore, expenditure of time and money on accident prevention is justified. Another point is that the victim may sue the organisation, if the injury has been a serious one. Although it seems to be customary for damages in cases of industrial accidents to be settled only years later, which means that the individual suffers in the interim, the sums involved can be staggering, perhaps even threatening to the organisation's survival.

Ask yourself, how many people are involved when an industrial accident occurs? Here is a selection:

- the victim
- the victim's workmates
- the first-aid person
- the personnel officer
- the safety officer
- the members of the safety committee
- the works manager
- the safety representatives
- the ambulance personnel
- doctors, nurses and other staff at the hospital
- national insurance staff
- the factory inspector
- union officials
- the victim's family, dependants and relatives
- last, but not least, you — the victim's supervisor

The list is pretty formidable, and it could be added to. The total cost to the organisation alone of a single lost-time accident probably runs into four figures — especially when you take into the account the fact that the person will be off work for at least a while. Multiply such sums of money by all the accidents in the country, and the total is mind-boggling.

Almost always an accident has at least four components:

- faults of persons — things for which they may rightly be blamed or held responsible
- unsafe acts or conditions — the results of faults or persons
- accidents — the results of unsafe acts or conditions
- injuries — the results of accidents

Whenever you are investigating an accident, it is a good idea to work backwards until you find the root cause. Too often, supervisors who discover the individual whose ultimate fault the accident was simply bawl them out or perhaps even fire them. This is not constructive. What you should aim to do is to correct the action — not the person — and fix the problem rather than beat the person over the head with the blame.

Most of us would prefer to prevent an accident rather than deal with it afterwards. Remove the first two components in the list above and, quite obviously, components three and four can never happen. There are three fields in which you can pursue the reduction and prevention of accidents: the work area, the work method, and the workers themselves.

Think of some of the things in the work area that need your attention: storage and stacking, clear passages and exits, moving objects, surfaces and edges, good housekeeping, defective heating and lighting, poor ventilation, firmness of fixtures, access to fire appliances, and the condition of floors, roof and walls. Your company, in defining its organisation and safety policies, will have set up safety committees, who will meet regularly. One of their main tasks will be to get everybody who works in a certain area to realise that they should be on the alert for the dangers that, unless checked, inevitably creep into the workplace. No one in the work area can afford to take the attitude that such things can be left to other people: safety is the responsibility of everybody.

The next field for consideration is the work method. Be on the lookout for poor maintenance, defective tools and materials, poor or untidy layout, defective safety guards and deficiencies in protective equipment and clothing. As with the hazards related to the work area, it is essential that everyone is vigilant about the dangers created by working methods, but there is a further responsibility on you as supervisor. Whenever a new method of doing a job is instituted, a piece of new machinery is installed, or a new worker joins the team it is essential that a step-by-step procedure is carried out to show explicitly to everyone concerned the what, the how and the why of the things that are to be done. For example, if someone changes their mode of working without authority, it is inevitably because they think that there are benefits, either personal or organisational, to be derived — a person might move a safety guard so that they can work more quickly. It is up to you to detect such changes and explain to the person that the potential losses far outweigh any possible benefits. (Unless, that is, they do not: it is always possible that the employee's idea is a good one.) Clearly the designers of machinery should consider their possible misuses and build in safeguards against them occurring, but you too should look carefully at any new piece of equipment and satisfy yourself that it is truly safe.

Training of new workers must always be done with care, but especially so in the realm of safety. New employees are particularly vulnerable to accidents because, all too often, they have been told what to do but not shown in detail exactly how to do it, and why it is done in that particular way. Whoever does the training, it is important that he or she is capable of communicating the necessary knowledge effectively.

This brings us to the third field, safeguarding the individual worker. Here we are concerned about such matters as personal attire, general conduct, morale, the use of protective clothing and devices and the individual way of working — all of which can present a safety hazard. If they are not to do so, there is one thing that is more important than anything else: training.

The responsibility for ensuring that your new recruits are trained for safety is yours. Even if managers further up the ladder are uncooperative — they may be living in the past and think that training is a waste of time and money — you must give every new recruit the most thorough safety-training course it is within your power to give.

As a supervisor, you will be setting an example, either good or bad, to your team. Make sure that the example you set is a good one by taking all the safety precautions available for every job. Even so, it must be stressed to the team that they, too, are responsible for safety: a family row over breakfast or a shouting-match with another driver on the way to work can easily induce a 'couldn't care less' attitude or a powerful mood of aggression towards inanimate objects or other team members. Or, if the weather is hot, people may be tempted to forego safety clothing. It is always so easy to become careless and find an excuse to justify not thinking about that little extra effort required to ensure safe working. A single, small unsafe act can be repeated until it has become an unsafe habit.

Every unsafe act is a challenge. As a supervisor, you should regard it as an opportunity to show that you mean to have the safety regulations observed in your department. After all, if you see a dangerous act and do nothing about it, and the culprit knows this, how can you expect the members of your team to be safety-conscious?

As we have seen, the way to prevent accidents is to nip them in the bud by correcting faults of persons, by forestalling repetition of unsafe acts and by doing something about unsafe conditions. One way to help is to prepare job-guidance sheets. These should have three columns, headed something like 'what to do', 'how to do it' and 'why do it this way?'. For example, if you were instructing someone on how to hammer a nail into a piece of wood you might put as the first entry in the 'what to do' column: 'Place wood on bench.' Beside this, in the 'how to do it' column, you might write: 'On an even surface.' Finally, under the 'why do it this way?' heading you could explain: 'To prevent slipping and avoid injury to hand.' The same pattern can be adopted through every single stage of hammering a nail into a piece of wood. To compile such a sheet the best thing to do first is to analyse the particular job to produce a list of every stage in it: this will be the basis of your 'what to do' column. Think hard about this: make sure you haven't missed out any stages because they are so glaringly obvious to you that you forget they may not be obvious to a new recruit. Once the first column has been compiled, you can go back through all the steps, writing in the 'how' beside each entry in the first column, and finally you can fill in the third column, the explanations of why each thing is done this way. If you find at this stage that, on occasion, you cannot think of a good reason why something is done in the way you have prescribed, then it is worth asking someone else and, perhaps, thinking about changing the way the job is done.

Preparing a job-guidance sheet reminds you of the essential points you want to put across to the learner so that he or she is able to do the job efficiently, safely and more quickly. Of course, it would be a never ending task to prepare job-guidance sheets for every single task done in the department so, to help relieve the pressure, it is worth classifying the jobs in terms of health and hazard, and then tackling first the ones where the risks are greatest. Do not be tempted just to cope with the obviously dangerous ones and then sit back smugly, believing that you have done all you need to do. You should work your way as far down the list as is practicable.

Making the environment safe

The environmental aspect of safety can be taken as covering the whole area of the plant itself, the equipment and the materials used. It is a complex business, making a plant safe and keeping it that way, and it requires a planned procedure of inspections and checks. However, you will not even get off the ground unless you are aware of all the possible sources of danger, a selection of which we shall discuss below.

The physical building itself can contain hazards: unexpected dangers abound in factories, workshops, storerooms and offices. A few examples are unsuitable floors or floors in serious disrepair, badly maintained stairways and gangways, sudden changes in floor levels, dangerous openings such as lift-shafts, protruding edges and insecure fixtures.

Then there is the machinery being used. The main hazards of machinery are at the point of operation, and from belts and pulleys, gears, projecting parts, shaft ends, clutches and other moving parts. Guarding devices should be such that they prevent access to the dangerous parts while the machine is in motion or, if this is not possible, should incorporate an automatic device to stop the machine before the operator can come into contact with the dangerous part. Interlocking devices should be included to prevent the removal of a guard while a machine is in motion. You should also give consideration to safe methods of maintenance.

Contamination of the air through bad ventilation results, in some organisations, in serious cases of illness. Also, where inflammable vapour and dust are present, there is the risk of explosions. The best preventive is to find less harmful substitutes for potentially toxic or otherwise dangerous materials; if this is impossible, efforts need to be concentrated on the removal of harmful substances as near to the source as possible. A less obvious effect of bad ventilation is that it increases accidents through people having difficulty concentrating on the job in hand. Of course, you may not have the authority to change your department's ventilation system; if not, go to as senior a manager as you need to to see that something is done about it.

Lighting has its effects on safety, too. Obviously you want to make sure that the lighting at the point of operation is good, but to many people it is less obvious that so should be the overall quality and amount of light in the department. Glare and lack of uniformity are as serious sources of danger as straightforward dimness.

The dangers of defective lifting machines and tackle are horrifying, but they are often ignored in factories, warehouses and building sites. Regular examinations are only part of the necessary drill. You must be absolutely certain in your own mind that the maintenance of all such equipment is in the hands of completely reliable people; also, you should be satisfied that the equipment is not deteriorating because of poor storage arrangements. Even lifting machines and tackle that are mechanically sound can cause accidents if they are used carelessly or handled by untrained operators.

It is unusual for British industry to suffer fewer than 30 fatalities per year through accidents with electricity. Many electrical accidents are due to faulty equipment — worn plugs and cables, wrongly coloured leads, defective earthing, temporary wiring, and so on. A high proportion of the accidents occur to people handling portable equipment.

Electric and power machines in fact cause fewer accidents than nonmechanical equipment, perhaps because we have more respect for them. Hand tools alone account for nearly 7 per cent of all reported accidents, the most frequent culprits being hammers, spanners and knives. One area of particular concern is the 'handy' improvised tool: it can be quite literally lethal.

An untidy workplace is an unsafe one. Workers are distracted from what they are trying to do through constantly having to stop short and search for the next thing they need. Obstacles lie around just waiting to be fallen over or bumped into. Rickety stacks of boxes or other items topple over. The waste generated by any particular process should be disposed of, since by adding to the clutter it can cause accidents. Moreover, there is a psychological aspect involved: there is little doubt that a clean, tidy and well decorated workplace induces in people a good attitude towards safe working.

Finally, there is fire. The risk of it breaking out can be minimised by eliminating unnecessary sources of ignition and surplus accumulations of inflammable materials. In addition, it is important that fire-fighting equipment be well maintained and appropriate, and that there are well trained people always available to use it. Obviously there should be an adequate means of escape, and all employees should know what to do in case of fire. Fire drills are essential as a training tool, but they should not be too frequent: people can become so blasé about fire drills that, when a real fire breaks out, they think it is just another drill and react sluggishly to the alarm bells.

In sum, no matter how many years of experience we have in our jobs, it pays to sit back and look at our methods to see if they can be improved. The time taken in establishing safe systems at work will be more than amply repaid in terms of all the benefits accruing over the years:

- fewer man-hours lost through accidents
- increased morale
- increased production

And never must we forget the humanitarian aspect. If someone loses a limb or their life because you, their supervisor, simply couldn't be bothered to think about safety, your conscience will torment you until your dying day.

Motivation for safety

How best can you motivate your team to ensure that they, too are concerned about safety? Basically, you must always remember that a key factor in motivation is to point out the benefits involved in the thing you are asking the person to do. For example, if you say 'Use the safety guard' you are telling the person the right action to take. However, if you say 'You are less likely to lose your fingers if you use the safety guard' you are pointing out the benefit to the person of doing what you say — and you are putting the benefit first. You are stressing what is in it for the listener.

It is often difficult to remember to state the benefits: they are so obvious to you that you assume that they will be obvious to any damn' fool. The trouble is that often they are not. Imagine that you were issuing safety shoes, and said: 'These safety shoes are made of strong leather and have toecaps of one-eighth-inch steel. The sole is leather, a quarter inch thick, and the heels are reinforced.' The chances are that the listener's mental reaction would be: 'Those shoes must be hot and heavy. They'll hurt my feet and I'll get tired.' Whenever possible the person will try to dodge out of wearing the shoes. Instead, you might have said: 'To protect your feet and save you pain and misery, it is a good idea to wear these safety shoes. To give you the protection you require, they are made of strong leather and have good solid toecaps. The heels are reinforced and the leather in the soles is a quarter of an inch thick.' The likely response of the person is to be impressed by all the same pieces of information which originally made the shoes seem such an unattractive option.

Presentation of ideas is important. If you put on a garment in the morning, glance in the mirror, decide you look awful, and therefore change into a different garment, that is fine. But supposing that instead it is your spouse who takes one look, winces and says: 'That's appalling. Change into something else.' Your natural response is to insist on staying dressed the way you are. But if your spouse says 'Don't you think you'd look better in the red one?' you will probably agree. The first version of your spouse's comment simply said you had made an error of judgement; the second contained an expression of the benefits to be received by changing out of the offending garment.

So simply imposing safety standards will have little effect on motivating your people to take care — if anything, accidents are likely to increase slightly because people will resent being ordered about. However, if you always point out the benefits both to the individual of doing this rather than that, or simply of not doing that, they are not only more likely to suffer less risk of accidents at the workplace but will probably respect you all the more for being the effective supervisor you have become.

CONCLUSION

Of all managers the supervisor is closest to the people who actually do the work and — more often than not — closest to the customer. Therefore the development of effective supervision is a matter of paramount importance. A company that is aiming for excellence can do no better than to invest time and money training its supervisors along the lines advocated in this book.

Apart from acquiring through thought and practice the core skills of leadership, motivation and team-building, communication and creative problem-solving, the effective supervisor will also have clear policies and up-to-date information on personnel procedures, such as the system for disciplining those who fall short of required standards, and industrial relations. This book, which draws upon many years of experience by The Industrial Society in identifying and teaching best first-line management practice, gives you in a nutshell the key elements of that professional knowledge.

Yet being an effective supervisor is more than knowing what to do and how to do it; it transcends knowledge of systems and procedures. Ultimately it is what you are as a person. Your qualities of mind, personality and character will colour your actions. If you think of the really impressive managers you have known they are persons of integrity, consistent but flexible and open to new ideas, enthusiastic and warm-hearted, tough but fair, calm and cool in crisis, and caring for those in need.

That may sound a tall order! But becoming an effective — or more effective — supervisor is not an easy task. It is a challenge, one that can last for your whole career. For it is comparatively easy to achieve initial success as a leader. The test is whether or not you can sustain leadership over a long period, in difficult circumstances and with a changing team. Can you go on growing in the quality and depth of your contribution as a first-line leader? Too many supervisors confuse progress with promotion. Do not misunderstand me: the latter is often welcome. But there is still

126

a challenge for the older, more experienced supervisor, who has been in his or her post for many years. For none of us has yet conquered the highest peaks of team leadership. There is always more to be learnt, more knowledge of the job, the business and more personal and transferable skills to be mastered.

This book will have failed if it has not struck that note on the trumpet. I trust that the action points that you have written down while reading it will provide you with an agenda for turning common sense into common practice. Whatever the organisation you work for does or does not do, whatever the other supervisors are like, you can resolve to get your bit right. For you may recall the old proverb which says, 'If you are not part of the solution you are part of the problem.'

INDEX

potential 80
Manual workers and absenteeism 57
Mass communication 22, 24, 25, 27
Materials (safety) 122, 124
Measurement of absenteeism 50-2, 60, 61, 63, 70
Medical advice 71
Medical incapacity 50
Methods of communication 22
Methods of working 35, 81
Misconduct 35, 39, 45
Monitoring
communication 29
delegated tasks 16
induction programme 75, 78
performance 16, 92
productivity 20
safety 122
standards 48
Morale 48, 97, 117
Motivation 46
political 12
safety 124-5

National Examination Board for Supervisory Studies 94
National Insurance 57
Needs
individuals 7, 8
teams 7
training 10
Negotiation, procedures 114
New rules 36
New staff
induction 72, 74, 77
safety 76, 120
teams 77, 78
Newsletters 27
Non-union firms 103, 106
Notice boards 24, 26
Notification of new supervisor 93

Objectives
employers' 2, 4, 5, 8, 10, 33-4
teams 6, 8
Occupational health 69, 71
Offenders 40, 43, 44
Offices 56, 82, 122
Shops and Railway Premises Act 1963 116
On-the-job training 11
Organisation of work 62
Organisations
size 55
structure 8, 78, 86, 99
Orientation of new staff 74
Outside activities 90
Overtime 51, 57, 78

Participation *see* **Involvment**
Patterns of absenteeism 52
Pay 76, 77
shop stewards 114, 115
supervisors 111
Pay *see also* **Wages**
Pension schemes 27, 75, 76, 78
People as a resource 12, 72, 85
People-oriented supervisors 98-9
Performance 9, 16, 48, 92
Persistent absentees 64, 66, 68
Personnel department
disciplinary procedure 37
health functions 71
induction 75, 76, 78
Plant bargaining 111-2
Policies 2, 3, 4, 55, 119
Post Office
absenteeism survey 53, 66
immunisation programme 70
Praise 9, 56, 61, 62
Probationary period 16, 63
Problem-solving 9, 13
Procedural agreements 109, 110
Procedures